AF588450

Demetrius the Besieger and the Wars of Alexander the Great's Successors

Demetrius the Besieger and the Wars of Alexander the Great's Successors

Simon Elliott

Pen & Sword
MILITARY

First published in Great Britain in 2026 by
Pen & Sword Military
An imprint of Pen & Sword Books Limited
Yorkshire – Philadelphia

ISBN 978 1 39906 988 5

A CIP catalogue record for this book is available from the British Library.

Typeset by Mac Style
Printed in the UK by CPI Group (UK) Ltd, Croydon, CR0 4YY.

The Publisher's authorised representative in the EU for product safety is Authorised Rep Compliance Ltd., Ground Floor, 71 Lower Baggot Street, Dublin D02 P593, Ireland.
www.arccompliance.com

For a complete list of Pen & Sword titles please contact:

PEN & SWORD BOOKS LIMITED
47 Church Street, Barnsley, South Yorkshire, S70 2AS, England
E-mail: enquiries@pen-and-sword.co.uk
Website: www.pen-and-sword.co.uk
or
PEN AND SWORD BOOKS
1950 Lawrence Road, Havertown, PA 19083, USA
E-mail: uspen-and-sword@casematepublishers.com
Website: www.penandswordbooks.com

To my fantastic son Alexander, a lover of all thinks ancient and military, and a great tabletop warrior. Just like his dad!

Contents

Introduction

Demetrius was tall and his face was so handsome that they only marvelled, and not one of the sculptors and painters could achieve complete resemblance, for his features were both charming, and impressive, and formidable. Youthful courage combined with some indescribable heroic strength and royal grandeur. And his disposition was about the same, instilling in people both horror and, at the same time, ardent attachment to himself. In the days and hours of leisure, over wine, among pleasures and everyday activities, he was the most pleasant of interlocutors and the most pampered of kings, but in the business of war he was persistent, tireless and stubborn like no one else. (*Parallel Lives*, Demetrius, 2.2)

Here Plutarch describes Demetrius Poliorcetes, the besieger of cities, a true giant of the Hellenistic world. A man at once exuberant and charismatic, yet deeply flawed. A warrior, general and king who came closest in terms of character and temperament to matching Alexander the Great. They certainly looked alike, given that busts of the pair are often indistinguishable.

Alexander was a great believer in divine heroism. Many of his battles were won through insane bravery and sheer strength of will. In Demetrius, he had a kindred spirit. The one man who, briefly, relit the spark of Hellenism as a force of enlightenment and philanthropy, even if his dalliance with Athenian democracy had more to do with furthering his own cause than altruism. Further, in founding the Antigonid dynasty in Macedon, Demetrius directly linked the world of Alexander with that of mighty Rome, the nemesis which ultimately crushed the Hellenistic kingdoms in the eastern Mediterranean one by one. Indeed, to the Romans, Demetrius was second only to Alexander as the model heroic leader. Glamorous, sometimes bad, dangerous to know, and ultimately doomed. As was his Roman counterpart in their volume of Plutarch's *Parallel Lives*, the dashing Mark Antony.

Despite a lifetime defined by military success (for the most part), it was in Demetrius' private life that his flaws came to the fore, just as with Alexander. Here the first-century BC Greek historian Diodorus Siculus says:

> He had an arrogant spirit and pride, and looked down not only on ordinary people, but also on those of the royal class, and what was most characteristic of him, in peacetime, was that he devoted all his time to drunkenness and feasts, which were accompanied by dancing and revelry, and in general, imitating Dionysus.[1]

Here we have another link with Alexander, also associated in his lifetime with the Greek god of winemaking, revelry and fertility. As Romm says, when not occupied in the business of industrial scale killing on the battlefield, both enjoyed 'wine-soaked binges, sexual escapades, and riotous loose living'.[2] Indeed it is no surprise that, at the end of his life as a pampered-though-depressed captive of Seleucus, Demetrius most likely drank himself to death.

Chapter Flow

The story of Demetrius is complex, his life a true enigma of immense highs and plunging lows. To help the reader follow his fantastical journey I have kept the structure of the book as simple as possible.

First, after this short introduction, I provide a glossary of key terms and a timeline to help the reader follow Demetrius' travels through the Hellenistic world. Chapter 1 then covers Hellenistic warfare in depth, given the story of Demetrius is one of relentless military conquest. Next,

Chapter 2 provides a pen portrait of the later Classical Greek world, the rise of Macedon under Philip II and the campaigns of Alexander. Their stories are an integral part of this narrative given they set the scene for the rise of the Antigonids. Indeed, in this chapter I also tell the story of Demetrius' family and, after his birth in 337 BC, his early life. This was framed by his father Antigonus Monophthalmus' key role in Alexander's conquest of the mighty Achaemenid Persian Empire. Chapter 3 begins with the death of Alexander in a blistering Babylonian summer in 323 BC and the subsequent implosion of his empire as his leading commanders strove to seize the Macedonian throne. Here I cover the First and Second Wars of the Diadochi (Successors). In the latter, Demetrius first made a name for himself on the battlefield as a mighty warrior, fighting alongside his father Antigonus against their archrival Eumenes of Cardia. This included Demetrius playing leading roles as a young man in the crucial battles of Paraitacene and Gabiene in modern Iran.

Their ultimate success set Antigonus and Demetrius on the path to inherit much of Alexander's empire in Asia. However, a mighty rise often leads to a mighty fall, and so it was here. As I detail in Chapter 4, they spent the next fifteen years fighting their Successor challengers in the Third and Fourth Wars of the Diadochi. The latter included Demetrius' year-long siege of Rhodes, the event which earned him his 'Poliorcetes' (the Besieger) sobriquet. For much of this time they were in the ascendancy, with Demetrius winning a series of conflicts in the Levant, Greece, Macedonia and Cyprus. However, the crushing defeat of Antigonus and his son at the Battle of Ipsus in 301 BC, where the former perished fighting with his phalanx at the age of 81, brought their supremacy to a crashing end.

From that point Demetrius was on his own, though if anything he became even more ambitious. In Chapter 5 I detail how he rebuilt his army and navy in Cyprus, soon becoming the king of Macedon (setting in place the Antigonid dynasty there), but then had to flee the coterie of Successor rivals who once more ganged up on him. Arriving in Greece, he then appointed his son Antigonus II Gonatas to manage Antigonid interests there, providing the platform which enabled the latter to eventually regain the Macedonian throne. The Antigonids then ruled the kingdom until the final defeat of Perseus by the Romans at the Battle of Pydna in 168 BC. For Demetrius himself, there was one last throw of the dice. At the end of the chapter I detail his planned *anabasis* in 287 BC when, in true Dionysian fashion, he launched an invasion of the eastern Hellenistic world. If he had succeeded, he would have truly been following in Alexander's footsteps. Sadly, for Demetrius it was a gamble too far. After initial success in the face of far superior numbers, he abandoned his plans on the borders of Syria. There he was captured by Seleucus in 286 BC, dying in opulent captivity in 283 BC at the age of 53.

Finally, in my conclusion I detail how Demetrius' Antigonid legacy in Macedon crumbled in the face of the relentless rise of Rome as the Hellenistic kingdoms in the eastern Mediterranean fell one by one. The book finishes with two appendices. The first provides pen portraits of the leading successors as a point of reference for the reader. The second covers the battles of Alexander the Great given they are often referenced in the context of the campaigns of Antigonus Monophthalmus and Demetrius. Finally, I have a full Bibliography and Index.

Housekeeping

First, the geographic focus of the book. Here I consider the widest possible battle space, effectively the entire Greek known world in the aftermath of Alexander's death.

By necessity, I keep my focus on Demetrius as his story progresses, referencing events elsewhere if relevant. That is particularly the case in the Third and Fourth Wars of the Diadochi, given Demetrius' personal focus on Greece while his father fought in Asia.

Next, dynastic nomenclature. In this work I reference the Antigonids frequently, both the family of Antigonus Monophthalmus and the Macedonian dynasty Demetrius established. Here, I make clear which I am referencing in each case. Antigonid is the broader family, Antigonid dynasty the Macedonian royal family. Further, Demetrius himself is variously known as Demetrius I Poliorcetes in classical Greek, and the modern translation Demetrius the Besieger. I simply call him Demetrius.

Meanwhile, understanding ancient world chronology is also important when reading this book. In particular, an awareness of the key periods in Greek history is useful. To start, we have the Mycenaean period from 1,650 BC through to the Late Bronze Age Collapse around 1,250 BC. Next the Dark Age/Geometric period through to the beginning of the ninth century BC. Then the Archaic period, which transitions into the Classical period from the later sixth century BC. Finally, we have the Hellenistic period from the death of Alexander the Great in 323 BC through to the sack of Corinth by the Romans in 146 BC.

Acknowledgements

Lastly, I would like to thank those who have helped make this biography of Demetrius possible. First, as always, Professor Andrew Lambert of the War Studies Department at KCL, Dr Andrew Gardner at UCL's Institute of Archaeology and Dr Steve Willis at the University of Kent (where I am an Honorary Research Fellow). All continue to encourage my research on the Greek and Roman world. Also Professor Sir Barry Cunliffe of the School of Archaeology at Oxford University, and Professor Martin Millett at the Faculty of Classics, Cambridge

University. Finally, my patient proofreader and amazing wife Sara. As with all my literary work, each has contributed greatly and freely, enabling me to complete this biography on the great Demetrius.

Thank you all.

Dr Simon Elliott
June 2026

Glossary

Achaemenid Dynasty	The ruling dynasty of the Achaemenid Persian Empire.
anabasis	Literally a 'march up', usually meaning a large-scale military expedition into the interior, particularly into the East.
Anatolia	Modern Turkey. I use Anatolia in preference to Asia Minor.
Antigonid Dynasty	The Macedonian dynasty established by Demetrius.
Antipatrid Dynasty	The Macedonian dynasty established by Cassander.
Argead Dynasty	The original ruling dynasty of Macedon.
Argyraspides	Later Macedonian and Hellenistic elite foot guards, named after their silver shields.
aspis	The standard, large round body shield used by Greek hoplites.
Attica	The large Greek peninsula projecting into the Aegean Sea, featuring Athens and its hinterland.
bireme	A war galley with two banks of oars.
Chalcidice Peninsula	The three-pronged peninsula in coastal northeastern Macedonia, today called the Halykydiki Peninsula.
Chalcolithic period	The Copper Age.

chiliarchia	A unit of organization for Macedonian and Hellenistic troops.
combined arms	Coordination of the various branches of the military.
cuirass	Rigid armour for the torso, usually consisting of breast and back plates.
dekad	A file of Macedonian phalangites, originally 10 deep after the reforms of Philip II, later 16 deep.
democracy	A system of government in the Greek *poleis* where the whole population (or at least those eligible to vote) elect their ruling officials.
Diadochi	The successor generals fighting for control of all or part of Alexander the Great's empire after his death, for example Demetrius.
doru	A hoplite's long thrusting spear.
embolus	The wedge-shaped formation used by Macedonian and Hellenistic shock cavalry.
Euboea	The large Greek island running along the eastern side of the Balkans peninsula from Central Greece to Attica.
galley	A key form of maritime transport in the ancient world, the galley featured oars along its length to provide the power to propel the vessel through the water in addition to, or instead of, a sail.
greave	Shin guard, usually sheet metal.
Hellenistic	The period of Greek history from the death of Alexander the Great to the rise of Roman power in the eastern Mediterranean.

Hetairoi (Companions)	A unit designation originating from the Macedonian king's close bodyguard cavalry. By Alexander's reign the title was extended to all the Macedonian regular heavy cavalry, with the Ile Basilike (Royal Squadron) forming the king's elite guard cavalry. During Demetrius' time such bodyguard units were known as *agema*.
hipparchia	A unit of organisation of Macedonian cavalry.
hippeis	Spartan knights, the elite troops among the Spartan army. Singular is *hippeus.*
hoplite	The principle line-of-battle warrior in the armies of the Greek *poleis.*
Hypaspists	Shield Bearers. Macedonian elite foot guards.
Iphicrates	Athenian general of the early fourth century BC whose reforms of line-of-battle foot included lighter armour, smaller shield and a longer spear.
ile (plural *ilai*)	Unit of organization for Macedonian cavalrymen.
Immortals	Elite guard troops of the earlier Achaemenid Persian kings.
Ionian	A dialect of ancient Greek, particularly among the Greek colonial cities in western Anatolia.
kopis	A slashing sword with an inwardly curved blade, extensively used in the Classical world.
lambda	The upturned V symbol used by the Spartans. The Greek equivalent of the letter 'L', it stood for Lakadeimon, the Spartan state.
Magna Graecia	The region settled by Greek colonists in southern Italy and Sicily.

mahout	An elephant rider controlling the animal, sitting astride its neck.
oligarchy	A form of autocratic rule by a few individuals, the common alternative to democracy in the Greek *poleis*.
panoply	The arms and armour of an ancient warrior.
Peloponnese	The large peninsula located at the southern tip of the Greek mainland.
peltast	A lighter type of Greek warrior armed with javelins, ideal for use in difficult terrain.
pelte	The smaller, round shield used by Iphicratean hoplites and, later, Macedonian and Hellenistic phalangites.
perioikoi	Spartan hoplites recruited from the city's hinterland.
pezetairoi	Macedonian line pikemen armed with a *sarissa*.
phalanx	A dense, organized body of spear- or pike-armed heavy infantry.
polis	Greek city-state (plural *poleis*)
prodromoi	Macedonian lance-armed light cavalry
Punic	A word used to describe Carthaginian armies and territory.
psiloi	The lightest type of Greek warriors, best suited to skirmishing with missile weapons.
pteryges	A skirt of leather strips worn to protect the groin and upper thighs.
Ptolemaic Dynasty	The dynasty of Hellenistic rulers established in Egypt by Ptolemy I.
Sacred Band	The elite group of 300 paired hoplites in the Theban army.

sarissa	The Macedonian and Hellenistic pike, held two-handed towards the rear.
satrapy	A Persian province goverened by a Satrap.
Seleucid Dynasty	The dynasty of rulers established in much of Alexander the Great's former empire by Seleucus I, including most of the Middle East, the east and occasionally much of Anatolia.
Spartiate	A Spartan citizen hoplite.
strategos	A senior Greek or Hellenistic military officer.
Successors	See Diadochi.
trireme	A war galley with three banks of oars.
xyston	A long lance up to 4m in length used by Macedonian and Hellenistic shock cavalry.
xystophoroi	Elite, *xyston*-armed Hellenistic shock cavalry.

Timeline

382 BC – Birth of Philip II of Macedon and Antigonus Monophthalmus (the One-eyed).
375 BC – Battle at Tegyra.
371 BC – Battle of Leuctra.
369 BC – Arrival of Philip II as a teenage hostage in Thebes.
362 BC – Battle of Mantinea.
359 BC – Philip II declared the full *basileus* (king) of Macedon.
357 BC – Philip II marries Olympias, daughter of the late Molossian king Neoptolemus, his fifth wife.
356 BC – Birth of Alexander the Great. Third Sacred War breaks out.
338 BC – Battle of Chaeronea.
337 BC – Birth of Demetrius I Poliorcetes.
336 BC – Assassination of Philip II, accession of Alexander the Great.
334 BC – Alexander the Great launches his *anabasis* eastwards, crossing into Asia. Battle of the Granicus River.
333 BC – Battle of Issus.
332 BC – Siege of Tyre begins.
331 BC – Battle of Gaugamela.
330 BC – Death of Darius III.
327 BC – Alexander the Great marries Roxanna.
326 BC – Battle of the Hydaspes River.
323 BC – Death of Alexander the Great.
322 BC – First War of the Diadochi begins.
318 BC – Second War of the Diadochi begins.
317 BC – Battle of Paraitacene.

315 BC – Battle of Gabiene. Death of Eumenes.
314 BC – Third War of the Diadochi begins.
312 BC – Battle of Gaza.
308 BC – Fourth War of the Diadochi begins.
306 BC – Demetrius I Poliorcetes conquers Cyprus.
305 BC – Demetrius I Poliorcetes begins his siege of Rhodes.
304 BC – Demetrius I Poliorcetes returns to Greece, styling himself a liberator and reinstating the Corinthian League.
301 BC – Battle of Ipsus, death of Antigonus *Monophthalmus*.
294 BC – Demetrius I Poliorcetes becomes king of Macedon.
288 BC – Demetrius I Poliorcetes forced off the Macedonian throne by Pyrrhus of Epirus and Lysimachus.
283 BC – Death of Demetrius Poliorcetes.
281 BC – Battle of Corupedium, death of Lysimachus.
281 BC – Assassination of Seleucus I by Ptolemy Ceraunus.
280 BC – Beginning of the Pyrrhic War in Italy with the invasion of Pyrrhus of Epirus.
274 BC – Beginning of the First Syrian War.
264 BC – Beginning of the First Punic War.
260 BC – Beginning of the Second Syrian War.
250 BC – Around this time the Bactrian satrap Diodotus declares his independence from the Seleucid Empire. Beginning of the Greco-Bactrian kingdom.
246 BC – Beginning of the Third Syrian War.
219 BC – Beginning of the Fourth Syrian War.
218 BC – Beginning of the Second Punic War, Battle of the Trebia.
217 BC – Battle of Lake Trasimene, Battle of Raphia.
216 BC – Battle of Cannae.
214 BC – Beginning of First Macedonian War.
202 BC – Battle of Zama, beginning of the Fifth Syrian War.
200 BC – Beginning of Second Macedonian War, Battle of Panium.

197 BC – Battle of Cynoscephalae.
192 BC – Beginning of Roman–Seleucid War.
190 BC – Battle of Magnesia.
172 BC – Beginning of Third Macedonian War.
170 BC – Beginning of the Sixth Syrian War.
168 BC – Battle of Pydna.
150 BC – Beginning of Fourth Macedonian War.
149 BC – Beginning of Third Punic War.
146 BC – Achaean War begins. Sackings of Carthage and Corinth.

Chapter 1

Warfare in the Hellenistic World

The Macedonian army of Philip II, Alexander and the Diadochi was pre-eminent in the age in which they lived. Time and again it proved supremely effective on campaign and in battle against the widest variety of opponents, ranging from the vast armies of Achaemenid Persia, the horse archers of the Asian steppe and the elephants and chariots of Indian armies.

Yet the story of how this supremely efficient military machine came into being is both lengthy and complex. Here I first look at the origins and function of hoplite warfare. This formed the bedrock of Greek military evolution, through to the time of Demetrius when hoplite heavy infantry were still much in use. I then move on to examine each arm of the Macedonian army created by Philip II, later used to such great effect by Alexander and the Diadochi. Central here was the creation of the *sarissa*-armed Macedonian pike phalanx which provided an anvil to pin the enemy main battle line, with the Macedonian shock cavalry the hammer which then broke it. Additionally, Philip II revolutionized siege warfare and naval combat. Both are also covered in depth here.

Hoplite Warfare in Ancient Greece

The term phalanx is used ubiquitously today to describe any dense body of organized spear or pike-armed infantry. However, it is most commonly associated with the hoplites and phalangites that came to dominate conflict in the Classical Greek and Hellenistic world. In the

Oxford Classical Dictionary, Hornblower and Spawforth say Homer was the first to use the term, in plural form to detail 'ranks' of soldiers.[1]

This was to differentiate their formal, organized form of combat from the individual duels he so often describes in the *Iliad* and *Odyssey*. Certainly, in the Minoan and later Mycenaean cultures through to the Late Bronze Age Collapse around 1,250 BC, highly organized, dense bodies of spearmen were a core element in the armies of the period. These were usually armed with long thrusting spears (called an *eka-a* by the Minoans) and tower body shields, later supplemented by enormous figure-of-eight shields. However, this style of organized warfare disappeared amid the economic catastrophe of the collapse, to be replaced by the individualistic style of warfare most associated with Homer.

Organized line-of-battle warfare in the Greek world only reappears with the onset of the Archaic period in the ninth century BC, when Hornblower and Spawforth say the term phalanx re-emerges (1996, 1153).[2] This time it is in the singular form we know today, being used to describe a totally new kind of warfare based on the newly emergent proto-hoplite. The first true Greek phalanx formations appear in artwork and literature after 700 BC, by which time they were playing a key role in the armies of the emerging Greek *poleis*. This very specific formation had its origins in two developments, one economic and one political.

- First, the re-opening of trade routes after the Greek Geometric/Dark Age. This led to the renewed establishment of colonies, for example in Italy, Anatolia and the Aegean Islands, increasing prosperity and thus the number of men within a city-state able to afford the full panoply of hoplite armour and weaponry. At this early stage such equipment was principally (if affordable by the individual) bronze body armour and a helmet, the *aspis* (plural *aspides*) large round body shield and the *doru* long thrusting spear. Early proto-hoplites could also be armed with javelins, perhaps reflecting the transition from the Geometric-style of individualistic combat to the far more organized form of warfare associated with the phalanx.

- Second, the emergence of the *polis* self-sufficient, autonomous state. This bound citizens more closely together within their communities than previously. Given that the first duty of the *polis* was to defend itself in time of war, this development was the catalyst to organize the fully armed hoplites into what became the classic Greek hoplite phalanx.

In such a formation the front rank troops usually fought with their long spears held in an overarm thrusting position (see discussion below), covered by interlocking *aspides* – large round body shields. Those at the rear added their weight to the formation, replacing those falling in battle at the front.

In terms of hoplite equipment, the most essential item was the *aspis* shield. This highly successful design had its origins in the bronze-faced and centrally gripped shields of the Urnfield culture that dominated central Europe from 1,300 BC to 700 BC. Here, the vectors of cultural transmission were the Dorian invasions of mainland Greece in the Geometric period. It therefore seems likely that the mature *aspis* design predated its use by hoplites in the traditional phalanx, with the first to carry them being the proto-hoplites of the later Archaic period.

The hoplite *aspsis* was a shallow bowl design between 80cm and 100cm wide. The wooden shield was completely covered in bronze sheet with an offset rim, featuring a double grip across the centre. Through this the left forearm was inserted, with a leather grip on the outer rim held in the left hand. This was a complex piece of military technology, expensive to make and requiring a variety of craftsmen of different skills to manufacture.

The characteristic domed shape of the *aspis* was vital to the successful functioning of the hoplite phalanx. Such shields were often brightly decorated, either to identify a given nationality (the best-known example is the Spartan *lambda*: Λ), to display martial valour, or to show overt wealth. Shields could also be fitted with leather or cloth skirts to protect the lower legs from arrows, these again often being decorated. Hoplite *aspides* were so successful they continued to be used until the disappearance of the traditional hoplite in the later third century BC, well after Demetrius' time.

The only major change in the shield used by hoplites was the limited replacement of the *aspis* by the *pelte*. This was a smaller, round shield faced in leather used by a new, lighter class of hoplite invented by Iphicrates, the great reforming Athenian *strategos*. He spent much of his life leading Athenian armies in the northern Balkans in the early fourth century BC. There he encountered opponents fielding predominantly light troops who were able to engage his battle-line hoplites from distance and then flee. To counter this he lightened the panoply of his hoplites with the smaller shield and lighter armour (see below). To compensate for the lesser protection, he gave them a longer (up to 4m) thrusting spear, effectively a proto-pike which could be used one or two handed. Thus was born the Iphicratean hoplite, an experiment that worked for Iphicrates at the time, though it was largely ignored by the other Greek *poleis*. Indeed, it was the Macedonians who paid the most attention, these new lighter hoplites effectively being a transitionary stage between the traditional hoplite and the Macedonian pike-armed phalangite.

For armour, proto- and early hoplites who could afford it wore a bronze cuirass known simply as a *thorax*, usually comprising a breast plate and back plate which gave significant protection to the warrior from the neck to the hips. Early designs were fairly primitive, the best known being the so-called 'bell cuirass', which dated to the later Archaic period. This was so named because of the distinctive bell-shaped marking across the pectorals. By the classical period these early designs had significantly evolved, with the most popular being the muscled cuirass made from hammered bronze plates, designed to replicate the muscles of the upper body. Boiled leather was also sometimes used to create the muscled cuirass design. However, by the time of Philip II, Alexander and Demetrius, only cavalry, officers and elite foot units wore such expensive armour, for example the foot guards of Agathocles of Syracuse.

By this time most hoplites who could afford armour wore a stiff linen or leather *linothorax* made from layers of material glued together to form a stiff shirt up to 5cm in thickness. Bronze or iron plates and scales could also be added to protect vital areas, for example the pectoral region or down the left and right sides where the chest and back plates were strapped together. Protective corselets made in this way often featured *pteryges* (meaning 'feather' in Ancient Greek) of layered linen or leather strips hanging from the base of the cuirass down to the thighs, these designed not only to provide additional protection for the lower abdomen and groin but also allow ease of movement. As with the *aspis*, corselets and *pteryges* were often brightly decorated, the former frequently with the head of a medusa to ward off the 'evil eye.' A fine example is that worn by Alexander in the Alexander Mosaic from the House of the Faun in Pompeii, the original now on display in the Museo Archeologico Nazionale di Napoli. Meanwhile, a final cuirass type had begun to appear in the early fourth century BC, this a lighter, quilted design of padded wool or cotton used by Iphicratean hoplites as detailed above.

Hoplite warriors also wore additional forms of armour, especially early on. These included hand, arm, thigh and foot guards, all made from bronze. However, by the classical period the most common type of additional armour was the bronze or iron greave sprung on the calf to protect the knee and lower leg. Later many hoplites replaced these with high leather boots, especially those equipped in the Iphicratean fashion.

The other key item of hoplite protection was the bronze (or less frequently iron) helmet, this evolving over time into a variety of popular designs. The earliest complex post-Mycenaean type found in Greece was excavated in a late Geometric-period grave from Argos in the Peloponnese, and was dubbed the Kegelhelm type. It comprised five pieces that together formed a cone shape covering the head and cheeks. Though the design had disappeared by the beginning of the seventh century BC, it had evolved into two further types called Insular and Illyrian. These, and their later developments, survived in use with hoplites through to the fifth century BC, mainly in the Peloponnese and the islands of the eastern Mediterranean.

However, by far the most successful Greek helmet design was the Corinthian type whose lineage led directly to the many fine forms of head protection common by the time of Philip II, Alexander and Demetrius. The earliest Corinthian design comprised a bronze domed bowl cast in two halves that provided full protection from crown to neck, with eyeholes either side of a nose guard and opening for the mouth. As with the Kegelhelm type, these early designs also dated to the late Geometric period, though from slightly later. This initial Corinthian design finally fell out of use in the eastern Mediterranean in the later fourth century BC, though it continued in use in Magna Graecia in Italy for much longer. There, it developed into a very specific type of head protection called the Italo-Corinthian helmet. This featured the eyeholes moving much further back towards the scalp to become decorative features, with this design remaining in use until the first century BC.

The main failing of all early Greek helmet designs was the lack of ear apertures to enable hearing. Because of this the Corinthian design eventually evolved into the Chaldicean helmet after 500 BC, when the first of these new types start appearing on vase paintings. This featured a much-revised bowl with earholes and elongated cheek guards that were sometimes hinged and sometimes not. The former later evolved into a further design called the Attic helmet which lacked a nose guard, this appearing from the fourth century BC and seeing extensive use in Magna Graecia.

The final evolution of the classic Greek hoplite helmet emerged at the beginning of the fourth century BC and is today called the Thracian (or Phrygian) type. This combined design features of the leather cap associated with Thracian warriors of all types with the Chaldicean helmet it resembled. The most notable difference was the use of even more pronounced cheek guards that often met at the chin to resemble a beard, and the appearance of a central ridge to provide additional protection across the crown of the head.

Additionally, two further types of helmet were worn by hoplites. Both were very popular by the time of Phillip II, Alexander and Demetrius, and evolved separately from the design lineages detailed above. The first was the Boeotian helmet, a protective development of the classic *petasos* wide brimmed Greek sun hat, with the sides folded down. This was an open design allowing good peripheral vision and unimpaired hearing, with a domed skull surrounded by a wide, flaring, down-sloping brim which at the rear came down to protect the back of the neck. Downward pointing folds either side provided minimal cheek protection. The Boeotian helmet was much used by Theban hoplites, and was also very popular as a cavalry helmet in Hellenistic armies given the excellent vision and hearing it provided.

Meanwhile, the Pilos helmet was a very simple conical design, based on the *pîlos* brimless Greek felt skull cap. A bronze version began to appear at the beginning of the fifth century BC, and by the time of Philip II, Alexander and Demetrius it was one of the most common forms of hoplite and phalangite head protection, being notably cheaper than more complex designs.

Greek hoplite helmets were often decorated with striking and distinctive crests. These were made from horsehair dyed as required then tied in bundles that were then slotted into holes cut into a crest box atop the helmet.

The primary weapon of the hoplite was the *doru* thrusting spear. This was usually 3 metres long, with the shaft (usually made from ash) tapering towards a small leaf-shaped blade of bronze or iron. At the rear a bronze spear-butt (*sauroter*) was attached, this often spiked for use if the primary blade was broken or to set the spear in the ground. The *sauroter* usually weighed around twice as much as the blade, moving the point of balance about two-thirds down the shaft, where a grip was fitted. Such weight distribution extended the reach of the spear and reduced its overhang at the back to prevent the warrior behind the front-ranker being stabbed as the weapon was drawn back.

The *doru* was usually held in the right hand above the shoulder. This enabled it to be thrust over the rim of the large *aspis*, though it could also be used to thrust underarm or set in the ground to receive a charge. Usually only one spear was carried by the hoplite, though spares were common in the baggage train.

A sword made from bronze or iron complemented the hoplite's *doru*. Types included the vicious looking *kopis* or *machaira,* featuring a forward-curving 60cm blade used for slashing, the *xiphos* short stabbing sword and the dagger-like Spartan *enchiridion*. Earlier, simple leaf-shaped sword blades were also popular.

Each *polis* and Classical Greek kingdom, including Macedonia, used the hoplite phalanx in different ways. Sparta, the most militaristic, treated its entire male citizen population as lifelong conscripts forbidden from any other work except soldiering. At the most elite level were the *hippeis* knights and Spartiate citizens, followed by the *perioikoi* who were recruited from the city's hinterland. Even Athens at its most democratic required all males between 17 and 59 to serve in times of war. Other *poleis* also had elite units within their wider hoplite formations, for example Thebes with the Sacred Band.

The depth of the hoplite phalanx was a matter of city-state preference and tactical expediency. Thucydides says the Spartan phalanx at the first Battle of Mantinea in 418 BC, when they and their allies defeated Argos, Athens and their allies, was eight deep.[3] This was also the standard depth for Athenian phalanxes, though other states such as Thebes often deployed their phalanxes much deeper, for example at the Battle of Leuctra in 371 BC, this clearly making an impression on the young Philip II when a hostage there. Leuctra also illustrates the increasing use of tactical innovation in phalanx warfare, with the Thebans deploying obliquely and withholding their centre and left flank while using an extra-deep right flank to great effect. This tactic of attacking with a strong wing, most often the right as above, while refusing another, was one which was readily adopted by Philip II, Alexander and their successors, and continued to be a major tactical feature on the battlefield throughout the Hellenistic period.

In terms of unit organization, hoplites formed up with a frontage and depth of 90cm per man, with each hoplite's right side protected by their neighbours projecting *aspis* shield. All of the above depths of formation were created by multiples of four men, though there is little evidence of any particular sophistication here outside of the Spartan army. However, in the case of the latter we have much detail thanks to Xenophon and his *Constitution of the Lacedaemonians*, dating to the beginning of the fourth century BC. This most organized of hoplite phalanxes was divided into six *morai*, each commanded by a senior officer called a *polemarch*. Below him were various officers of decreasing seniority, starting with four *lochagai*, then eight *pentecosters* and finally sixteen *enomotarchs*, the latter commanding a platoon-sized *enomotia* of thirty-six men. These were divided into three files of twelve, the *enomotarch* commanding the right-hand file with his second-in-command (*ouragos*) at the rear of the same file. The idea here was to ensure that every Spartan unit, no matter how small, had its own commander.[4] The much less complicated Athenian system from the same period featured ten regiments called *taxeis* of variable size, each drawn from one of the tribes of Athens and commanded by a *taxiarch*.

The experience of battle fighting as a hoplite is vividly described by the Spartan elegiac poet Tyrtaeus who wrote in the mid-seventh century BC. He says:

> Let each man stand firm with his feet set apart, facing up to the enemy and biting his lip, covering his thighs and shins, his chest and shoulders with the wide expanse of his shield. Let him shake his spear bravely with his right hand, his helmet's crest nodding fiercely above his head. Let him learn his warfare in the heat of battle and not stand back to shield himself from missiles, but let him move in close, using his spear, or sword, to strike his enemy down. Place feet against the enemy's feet, press shield against shield, nod helmet against helmet, so that the crests are entangled, and then fight your man standing chest to chest, your long spear or your sword in your hand.[5]

This highly evocative passage provides great insight into phalanx combat as experienced by the individual hoplite, weighed down carrying their *aspis* and *doru*, vision and hearing impeded by their helmet.

Hoplite engagements, whether against other hoplites or opponents armed differentially, began with a steady advance towards the enemy. The usual practice for citizen hoplites was to advance in loose order until in missile range when close battle order was adopted. Crowd psychology would then take over, no matter how well trained the warriors, with the speed of advance increasing given the desire of most hoplites to get the engagement over as quickly as possible, especially if under missile fire. At this point a key feature of hoplite combat would then become evident, this a prominent drift to the right as each warrior tried to take advantage of the protection offered by the adjacent *aspis*. This was exacerbated by the normal ancient-world practice of deploying the better troops on the right flank.

Around 200m from the enemy line the hoplites charged, shouting their battle cry. At this point, if their opponent had inferior morale and training, they might break. Assuming they didn't, the primary sources say the hoplites would now slow down to redress their ranks, giving the better trained troops a clear advantage from this point. Once the line was under control again, the final move to contact was then carried out, with combat joined. Against most contemporary opponents the tactics, weapons and armour of the hoplites then gave them a clear advantage unless against another hoplite force or, later, the Macedonian pike-armed phalanx. In the former case, when two hoplite battle lines clashed, a spear-duel ensued called the *othismos*, translating literally as 'to push'. Spears were thrust, aiming for the exposed faces and arms of opponents, with swords only drawn if the *doru* shattered.

One puzzle here regarding the *othismos* is how those pressing forward in the rear ranks didn't asphyxiate those fighting at the front. A modern rugby scrum is only three men deep for good reason, to preserve the physical integrity of those in the front row. Given the depth of hoplite phalanxes, some very deep in the later period as detailed, one would think that given the additional weight of armour and the press of each *aspis* into the backs of those in front, serious injury was unavoidable. The key factor here is that human beings need a minimum space around their thorax to expand their chests and breathe. To explain how the hoplite overcame this in the crush of phalanx combat, we can turn to experimental archaeology. Here, re-enactors using sports compression sensors have shown that the dome of the convex *aspis*, when positioned against the back of the man in front, leaves sufficient space to permit the man pushing to expand his thorax and breathe. Interestingly, the pressure sensor used in the experiments shows the extra pressure added by each new man in the file falls off sharply after eight ranks when the point of diminishing returns takes over. It is therefore probably no coincidence that eight men was the original preferred depth of a hoplite file.

At some point in the *othismos* one side would weaken and tire, with those towards the rear stumbling into a newly exposed space to be slaughtered if not fully aware of the situation to their front. Soon those at the very back, sensing the loosening cohesion at the front, would begin to flee, often discarding their weapons as they did. It is in this crucial phase of combat that the training, experience and morale of those fighting really came into play. Modern research into the behaviour of an average citizen (as opposed to a professional soldier) shows that most of the fighting and killing in combat is carried out by as few as ten per cent of those engaged. Once these are thinned through natural wastage in the fighting, the outcome is increasingly inevitable. The losing side will break.

Meanwhile, light troops formed an increasingly significant component of the armies of the Greek *poleis*. They are first recorded in use in Greek armies as early as the Persian invasion of Greece in 490 BC. Later, Athens is recorded deploying 800 archers at the Battle of Plataea in 479 BC during Xerxes' invasion.

Such troops can be categorized into two specific types. These are *peltasts* and *psiloi*. The former had their origins as hoplite servants, carrying the warrior's equipment on campaign. Their role evolved over time into fighting as skirmishers armed with javelins, with *psiloi* soon a catch-all term for all skirmishing light troops. These later included noted specialists armed with other weapons, for example Cretan archers and Rhodian slingers.

Tyrtaeus, in his elegiac poetry, vividly describes the role played by such light troops in battle, saying:

> And you, the light armed men, hiding behind the shields, launch your sling-stones and javelins at them, giving good support to the heavy infantry.[6]

Psiloi continued to develop and eventually led to the creation of the classic battlefield *peltast*. These were much better equipped with a wicker crescent-shaped version of the *pelte* shield and light helmet. Their primary weapon remained the javelin, which could be used at ranges of up to 60m. Increasingly *peltasts* were also equipped with a side arm. Meanwhile, one specific type of *peltast* stands out above all others, namely those recruited from Thrace. These are often depicted in contemporary imagery wearing their distinctive Thracian caps, and were renowned for their fierce charge, especially when armed with the vicious looking *rhomphaia*, a long-handled, two-handed cutting weapon.

Turning to cavalry in the age of the hoplite, these were very much an inferior component of Classical Greek armies, except in the various city-states of Thessaly. For much of this period the role of cavalry was largely scouting and skirmishing, though as part of the general trend towards *poleis* fielding more-balanced armies their role had increased by the beginning of the fourth century BC.

In contemporary artwork cavalry in the early hoplite period are generally shown equipped wearing a light panoply, perhaps only with helmet and shield. For offensive weaponry short spears and javelins were used, with a side arm if the mounted warrior could afford one. As time progressed this panoply improved, and by the beginning of the fourth century BC better off cavalry are shown wearing much improved protective equipment. For example, an early fourth century BC relief found at Thespiai in Boeotia shows a trooper in a bronze muscled cuirass flaring at the hip to allow free hip movement in the saddle, leather *pteryges*, Boeotian helmet (by now very popular with cavalry) and Thracian-style tall, leather boots. The weapons of this much-better-protected cavalryman remained the short spear and javelin, together with a side arm.

The ultimate example of these better-equipped cavalry were those from Thessaly, where access to its fertile coastal plains gave rise to a significant industry breeding fine quality cavalry horses in wealthy stables. This remained the case until the end of the Hellenistic period. Mounts raised here were much sought after regionally.

Heavy cavalry in the later hoplite period were organized in a variety of ways dependent on each individual *poleis*. For example the Greek allied cavalry that accompanied Alexander on the earlier stages of his *anabasis* were formed in five *ilai* of 128 men each. These deployed on the battlefield in a square formation sixteen horses wide and eight deep. Meanwhile, given their prowess, Thessalian cavalry were noted for more complex formations, for example the 1,800 who accompanied Alexander often deployed in a rhomboid formation led by their commander (*ilarch*) at the point closest to the enemy.

Even at this later stage, lighter-armed cavalry remained a component in the armies of the various *poleis*, either indigenous poorer troopers or allies and mercenaries. The latter included Thracians and Paeonians armed with javelin and bow, and highly sought-after Scythians known for their prowess in firing their bows from the saddle.

Foot Troops in the Age of Philip II, Alexander and the Diadochi

The composition of early Macedonian armies, for example those of Alexander I, Archelaus I and Amyntas III, reflected the kingdom's diverse geography and social structure. Thus, when on campaign and in battle, the principal arm comprised the king's retainer-based *hetairoi* (companion) cavalry and other mounted nobility. Foot units tended to be an unorganized collection of units based on tribal structure, either lowland peasants or highland herdsman, who were called to arms as required. Such troops were armed in a similar fashion to early Greek *psiloi* and *peltasts*.

It was Alexander I who created the first regular foot unit in the early fifth century BC with his *pezetairoi* (foot companion) guard regiment. These were trained and equipped as city-state hoplites. From this point, an increasing number of Macedonian foot were trained in this manner, though they, with the exception of the *pezetairoi*, proved less capable than their Greek counterparts to the south. Macedonian rulers made up for this by employing increasing numbers of experienced Greek mercenary hoplites when state finances allowed.

However, it is with the accession Philip II in 359 BC that a true revolution occurred in the Macedonian army, and one that played a crucial role in setting the kingdom on track to conquer their then-known world. This was the advent of the Macedonian phalanx armed with the *sarissa* pike, with all the pikemen now known as *pezetairoi*.

Philip was uniquely placed to facilitate this, and the other revolutionary changes he initiated, for two reasons. First, he had learned key lessons when a teenage hostage of the Thebans who were then the leading military power in Greece. Second, Philip as a ruler proved highly skilled at managing his kingdom's finances from the very beginning of his reign. He swiftly found means to raise the revenue to implement his military reforms.

Specifically on equipment, the key change in the defensive panoply of the Macedonian phalangite was with his shield. Gone was the *aspis* that prevented the use of a two-handed weapon. Its replacement was a development of the Iphicratean hoplite's *pelte* which retained the same name, though in this case was faced with bronze encasing a wooden core. The shield was 66cm in diameter based on examples found in archaeological excavations at Staro Bonče in the modern Republic of North Macedonia. Given that both hands were needed to wield the *sarissa*, it was hung on the left shoulder and held in place with a central arm grip for the left arm and a strap around the neck.

Macedonian *pelte* decoration was common in Hellenistic armies. The early shields of Philip and Alexander featured torches, thunderbolts, gorgon heads and the heads of Gods and heroes, together with the classic Macedonian star design. Later, notably in the reign of Demetrius, these were joined by monarchical portraits.

The armour panoply of the Hellenistic pikeman was similar to that of the late-Classical hoplite. Armour was usually of the linen *linothorax* variety, again sometimes reinforced with bronze or iron plates or scales. Bronze muscled cuirasses were worn by those who could afford them, usually officers.

The helmet of the *sarissa*-armed phalangite was again like that of later hoplites, with the advanced Thracian type popular with front rankers in the armies of Philip, Alexander and Demetrius. The simple *pilos* design was also popular, especially for those at the rear of the phalanx. The traditional Macedonian broad-rimmed *kausia* hat was worn on the march. Front rank troops were also the most likely to wear additional armour, for example greaves to protect their legs.

Aside from the *pelte* shield, it was the *sarissa* two-handed pike that differentiated the Macedonian pikeman from the *doru*-armed hoplite. Up to 5.5m long when first introduced, the *sarissa* had grown to 7.3m by the time the Macedonians later fought the Romans. It is not certain but in Demetrius' time it might have been around 6.5m long. The pike was usually made from ash, with *sarissa* fittings from a tomb at Vergina in northern Greece indicating the shaft was made in two pieces, with a 17cm-long iron tubular sleeve locking them together. This allowed the weapon to be dismantled for ease of carrying on the march. As with the *doru*, the *sarissa* featured a half-metre long, leaf-shaped, iron blade and a slightly shorter iron butt spike, both secured with hot pitch. The latter was significantly heavier than that used on hoplite spears given the role it had in helping balance the weapon, with the pike held using a handgrip towards the rear. The butt spike usually featured four 'wings' to steady the weapon when set in the ground. Meanwhile, again as with the hoplite, most pikeman also carried a sword.

Philip II's original pike phalanx formed in files ten deep, each known as a *dekad*. This had increased to sixteen by the time Alexander was on the throne, though the term *dekad* continued in use for the extended file. Alexander's expeditionary force of 12,000 Macedonian foot who accompanied him to Anatolia in 334 BC included 3,000 *hypaspist* ('shield bearer') guard troops (see later), and 9,000 *pezetairoi* foot companion phalangites. The latter were organized into six regionally-recruited 1,500-man *taxeis*, this representing around half of the overall total available in the Macedonian army. It seems likely that other *taxeis* of *pezetairoi* from the original Asian expeditionary force under Parmenion then joined Alexander after he arrived in Anatolia, though we have no detail of their number. Any remaining *taxeis* formed the core of the home army under the command of the veteran leader Antipater in Pella. Later, three of Alexander's *taxeis* were honoured with the title *asthetairoi* (possibly meaning 'closest companions') after showing great bravery at the Battle of Issus in 333 BC. Then, as Alexander's campaign against Persia continued, a further *taxis* of *pezetairoi* was added to his army in 330 BC, likely built around a core of veterans from existing units. Two further *taxeis* may have been added later for his Indian campaign, bringing the final total of *taxeis* at the time of Alexander's death to fifteen, or around 22,500 *pezetairoi*.

In Alexander's army each *taxis* was broken down into smaller units called *lochoi* (singular: *lochos*), though we have no idea of their exact strength. However, as the commander of each *lochos* was senior enough to attend Alexander's staff briefings when on campaign, *lochi* must have been significantly larger than a *dekad* file of 16 men. It seems likely that there were 6 *lochoi* per *taxis*, in which case each would be of 16 files, or 256 men, which gives a nominal strength of 1,536 men per *taxis*.

After Alexander's death the organization of the phalanx continued to evolve, not surprising given its complexity and the numerous individuals and kingdoms vying for superiority in the Wars of the Diadochi. This generated a true arms race that lasted through to the second century BC. An early change was the introduction of the *speria* that comprised two *taxis* in the better-trained formations of Demetrius and his rivals.

When arrayed for battle, the Macedonian *sarissa* phalanx could present the front five ranks of pikes lowered. These were held level at the waist, providing an impenetrable hedge of spear points. Those in the rear ranks then added their weight to the phalanx during the charge, replacing fallen comrades at the front as with the earlier Greek hoplite phalanx. The raised pikes of these rear-ranks formed a hedge that also broke up the impact of missiles fired at the phalanx. It is this Macedonian pike phalanx that led Polybius to comment on its imperviousness if tackled frontally in good conditions, saying:

> so long as the phalanx retains its characteristic form and strength nothing can withstand its charge or resist it face to face…we can easily picture the nature and the tremendous power of a charge by the whole phalanx, when it advances sixteen deep with levelled pikes.[7]

How did each phalangite use his *sarissa* to best lethal effect in such a cohesive formation? Christopher Matthew in his very useful discussion on the phalangite 'kill shot' explains that:

> It seems the long *sarissa*, held at waist level, was primarily used to hold an opponent in place, preventing him from reaching the phalangite with a shorter weapon like a sword or spear. In engagements where a pike-phalanx fought against another pike-phalanx, these same initial principles applied to both sides using their weapons to keep their

> opponents at bay. During the course of the encounter the phalangite would have continued to use his weapon in the same manner – pushing forward with the weight of his body and the weapon to both hold the enemy at bay and to probe his defences by slightly adjusting the position of the pike to try and move the opponent's shield out of the way or force them back. When this occurred, certain areas of the opponent's body would become exposed for a brief moment. At this stage the phalangite could either direct an attack towards the opponent's chest, or strike at the opponent's head.[8]

We know much more about the organization of the Macedonian pike phalanx than the Greek hoplite phalanx due to the late Hellenistic *Tactica* military manual of Asclepiodotus.[9] Dating to the first century BC, this may actually be a reproduced long-lost work by Posidonius of whom Asclepiodotus was a pupil. The latter was a sophist and historian who, Plutarch says, was a contemporary of the Macedonian King Perseus and who described the crucial Battle of Pydna in 168 BC which ended with Rome's final defeat of Macedon. Asclepiodotos' work is particularly useful given its focus not only on the phalanx but also other ancillary arms such as cavalry, light infantry and elephants.[10]

The *Tactica* and later manuals indicate the Macedonian pike phalanx was a step-change in complexity compared to earlier Classical Greek examples, featuring three densities of formation that were in use by the time of Demetrius. These were:

- Open order, with a frontage and depth per man of 1.8m and with no special name. This was the natural formation when deploying or manoeuvring.
- *Pycnosis*, with a frontage and depth half of that above and the usual formation when closing with the enemy in combat.
- *Synaspismos*, the locked shields formation with a frontage half of that used for *pyknosis* and double the depth. This was a purely defensive formation, it being used for example against Darius III's scythed

chariots at the Battle of Gaugamela in in 331 BC and in the later stages of the Battle of the Hydaspes in 326 BC.

One key point to consider regarding the Macedonian pike phalanx was the sheer number of men required to make the formation work effectively. While this was less of an issue for Philip II and Alexander on his *anabasis*, phalangite recruitment became increasingly problematic as the successor period progressed, and by the later Hellenistic period was a major issue. Indeed, although Perseus managed to raise a phalanx of 21,000 for his Pydna campaign against the Romans, this was only through an emergency socio-economic policy of requiring native Macedonians to beget more children.

A number of methods were used to compensate. For example, throughout the Wars of the Diadochi veteran troops were 'run on' for as long as possible, with Eumenes' Argyraspides fighting the Antigonids a good example, some of them probably fighting into their sixties at least. At the same time, native troops from the conquered territories were recruited and trained to fight in the Hellenistic military tradition, for example the Persians equipped as phalangites under Alexander. Later, both Antigonus Monophthalmus, Demetrius and Eumenes used similar *pantodapoi* phalangites, while the Ptolemies used native Egyptians trained as phalangites from the time of Ptolemy IV Philopator.

Meanwhile, Alexander's elite foot companions were called Hypaspists, the king taking 3,000 of them on his *anabasis*. The name derives from the ancient Greek for 'shield bearer.' Within the Macedonian military they were the only force not raised on a regional basis, this to ensure loyalty to the monarch given the feudal nature of the Macedonian state. Their exact origins are unknown, though it seems likely they evolved from Alexander I's original *pezetairoi* guards when the latter were greatly expanded by Philip II to become his new foot companion phalangites. A key point of difference seems to be the way they were armed, initially retaining the *aspis* and *doru* rather than re-equipping with *pelte* and *sarissa*.

Meanwhile, in contemporary imagery they are often shown wearing the finest defensive panoply, with Thracian helmets and high-quality cuirasses common, together with greaves.

The Hypaspists were organized into three units of 1,000, with Arrian saying that later in Alexander's reign these were styled *chiliarchia*.[11] This corresponds with the origins of the title *chiliarch* which Curtius says came into use after 331 BC.[12] One of the thousand-strong units was the senior, providing the king's bodyguards along with the seven close personal guards chosen from the companions and the royal pages. This unit of the Hypaspists was later known as the *agema*, and for the early part of Alexander's *anabasis* was commanded by Hephaestion.

From 327 BC a new term came into use for all Hypaspists. This was Argyraspides, based on their silver-plated shields.[13] Under this name, after Alexander's death they became the most sought-after unit in the Macedonian army, finally fighting for Eumenes. Following the latter's defeat by Antigonus Monophthalmus and Demetrius at Gabiene, where they proved a two-edged sword given their own success in the battle but subsequent betrayal of Eumenes, they were broken up as a unit and sent to the furthest corners of Alexander's former empire to live out their days as out-of-favour border guards. By the time of this 315 BC battle they were armed as elite phalangites with *sarissa* and *pelte*, and may have earlier been so equipped in Alexander's later campaigns too.

For other foot warriors, Philip II, Alexander and Demetrius all made good use of allied and mercenary troops. For example, when Alexander crossed into Anatolia to begin his *anabasis* his army included 7,000 allied and 5,000 mercenary Greek hoplites and *peltasts*, 7,000 Thracian and Illyrian *peltasts* and 1,000 other skirmishers. The latter included Agrianian javelinmen, Cretan archers and Rhodian slingers. Demetrius certainly made good use of locally recruited mercenary hoplites, *peltasts* and *psiloi*, these playing a key role in many of his campaigns.

Cavalry in Early Hellenistic Armies

Lance-armed shock cavalry were the hammer of the armies of Philip II, Alexander and Demetrius, with the phalanx being the anvil. They were originally called companions, and were first recruited from the leading aristocratic families in lower Macedonia, numbering around 800 horsemen. Though they initially fought in a similar manner to the mounted troops of the Greek *poleis*, from the early fourth century BC they had begun to charge to contact using long *xyston* lances up to 4 metres in length. The first to make the switch were the king's *hetairoi* close bodyguards, recruited from the companions.

Soon all squadrons of the companions followed, with the lance later giving its name to all Hellenistic shock cavalry, *xystophoroi*. By that time their numbers had greatly expanded, with each successor monarch maintaining the numbers in their own armies by encouraging Macedonian noble families to settle in their regions of control as colonists. Antigonus Monophthalmus and Demetrius were prime examples.

Macedonian shock cavalry usually wore a bronze muscled cuirass or linen/ leather *linothorax*, both cut for use on horseback, the latter often reinforced with iron plates or scales. As detailed earlier, an excellent example is that shown on the Alexander Mosaic in the House of the Faun in Pompeii, with its medusa head warding off the evil eye.

Unsurprisingly, here Demetrius went one better, having the master armourer Zoilus of Cyprus make for him two iron corselets for use when he besieged Rhodes. Both were immensely sturdy, weighing around 18kg, and could withstand a catapult bolt fired from twenty paces. This stands comparison to the shot-proof breastplates used by heavy cavalry in the European Renaissance.[14] Demetrius kept one for himself and gave the other to Alcimus of Epirus, a powerfully built officer tasked with leading his assault. Meanwhile, the Boeotian helmet remained very popular with Macedonian-style cavalry well into the Hellenistic period.

The armies of Philip II, Alexander and Demetrius also featured significant numbers of Thessalian and other Greek heavy cavalry fighting as allies and mercenaries. In addition, lightly armed skirmishing cavalry also featured, usually carrying javelins. These were often recruited from Thrace. Further east, they were joined by bow-armed skirmishers from the Asian steppe.

Elephants

Elephants were the most exotic and glamorous component of Alexander's later armies, and those of his successors. The Macedonian king first came across the beasts at Gaugamela in 331 BC when the Persian army included fifteen supplied by Darius III's Indian satrapies, with bowmen sitting astride their backs. However, whether they were used in the battle is debatable. Parmenion captured them when sacking the Persian camp after the battle, while twelve more came into Macedonian possession after the capture of Susa, according to Curtius.[15] There is no evidence any of these were incorporated in the Macedonian army at this time though.

Elephants then became a regular opponent of Alexander when he was campaigning in the Punjab, playing a prominent role in Porus's army at the Battle of the Hydaspes in 326 BC. By that time Alexander had already incorporated the first elephants into his own army, these supplied by Porus' rival, Taxiles of Taxila. Soon a fully-fledged elephant corps had been established in the Macedonian army with over 200 beasts. Their importance is well illustrated by a series of large silver coins struck in Babylon. These feature Alexander on horseback fighting Porus atop an elephant.

Alexander's early elephant corps retained their Indian fighting crew, though by the time of his death the bowmen had been replaced by a Macedonian pikeman.[16] This remained the case throughout the Wars of the Diadochi after the beasts had been distributed among the successor kingdoms. Demetrius himself used them at the Battle of Gaza in 312 BC and Ipsus in 301 BC. Elephants are notably long-lived, and these early Macedonian beasts lasted through to the reign of the Macedonian king Antigonus Gonatus (277 BC to 239 BC), Demetrius' son. Meanwhile, demand amid the Hellenistic successor kingdoms led to a thriving elephant trade with India, the Seleucid Empire being the main beneficiary. Indeed, an elderly Demetrius was to call Seleucus 'elephant keeper' by way of insult.[17]

Further west, as the original Macedonian elephant corps died out, smaller African forest elephants were used by Ptolemaic Egypt. These were sourced from the Horn of Africa after the Ptolemies were cut off from supplies of Indian elephants by the Syrian Wars against the Seleucid Empire.

Siege Warfare

Most Hellenistic leaders spent far more time engaged in siege warfare than set-piece battle. Demetrius was the best-known example, hence his nickname 'Poliorcetes' (Besieger of Cities).

The earliest type of Greek artillery was the *gastraphetes* belly bow, a simple crossbow-like device too powerful to be drawn by hand that could fire a heavy arrow up to 250m. It was invented by the military engineers of Dionysios I of Syracuse at the turn of the fourth century BC, with the bow itself comprising a composite of wood and sinew. This technology proved very scalable, and soon larger versions were developed. These were mounted on stands that used a windlass to draw the bow. They were called *katapeltes* ('shield piercer') in ancient Greek, this giving us the word catapult today. Further developments led to the specialized bolt-shooting *oxybeles* and the stone-shot-firing *lithobolos* or *petrobolos*, now better known by the Latin name *ballista*. The stone throwing engines tended to be larger than their bolt firing counterparts, a good example being that designed by Charon of Magnesia in the early fourth century BC, which had a 2.7m wide bow that could throw stone shot weighing 3kg. Later in the century, Isodorus of Abydos built a very large stone thrower that featured a 4.6m bow capable of firing an 18kg shot.

However, the defensive circuit walls of the Greek *poleis* still proved difficult to overcome. This all changed with the accession of Philip II in Macedon. As part of his military revolution, he hired Poleidus of Thessaly to take charge of a greatly expanded siege warfare capability. First, large numbers of bolt and stone throwers were built using existing technology. Then Poleidus began to innovate, for example building a series of 35m-high siege towers used when Philip besieged Perinthus in 340 BC. These were higher than the defensive towers of the town wall. Together with the use of newly developed rams mounted on rollers and skilled mining, they soon ensured the walls there fell to the Macedonians. Siege towers of this scale later became a favourite technology used by Alexander on his *anabasis*, often mounting artillery, and later by Demetrius. The latter is perhaps best-known for his Helepolis (City Taker), a 40m-high, iron-clad siege tower used when investing Rhodes in 305 BC.

Philip II's greatest siege warfare legacy, though, was the innovation of the torsion bolt-shooting catapult, and later the torsion stone thrower. Here the composite bow of the engine was replaced with two vertical springs made from sinew or horsehair set in wooden frames, with iron levers used to tighten them at the top and bottom. The springs were then further tightened as the arms were winched backwards, springing sharply forward into their original position once the trigger was released. Overnight this technology doubled the range of existing bolt-throwers, and later stone-throwing catapults too. Such weapons proved so successful that designs of all scales were soon created for use in siege warfare, and by the mid-third century Ptolemaic engineers had created a set of calibrated formula that set out the most effective dimensions for a torsion catapult firing a given size of bolt or stone, and the respective dimensions for each part of the weapon. By this time the acknowledged ideal size of stone ball for use against stone-built fortifications was 26kg, though the largest engines could throw a stone shot three times this size. Weapons of this size proved to be the elite military technology of the Classical world and weren't surpassed until the Byzantine adoption of the Chinese-developed trebuchet in the sixth century AD.

Naval Warfare in the Hellenistic Age

Nearly all campaigning theatres in the Classical world were dominated by access to the sea or major river systems. This meant that control of the open ocean, coastal littoral and riparian zones was vital to the success of military operations.

The main warship in the Classical world was the war galley. The first designs originated in the Greek Geometric/Dark Age period. These used a new maritime technology featuring locked mortise-and-tenon plank fastenings invented by the Phoenicians. This enabled true war galleys to be built for the first time, a technology that lasted through to the Renaissance period over 2,500 years later.

The first such war galleys were *monoremes* (i.e. featuring a single bank of oars) called *pentaconters*, with a bow-mounted ram on the waterline as the main weapon, alongside its fighting crew. By the time of the Greco-Persian Wars at the beginning of the fifth century BC they had been joined by *biremes* and *triremes*, the latter invented by the Corinthians around 530 BC. These were so called because they featured two and three banks of oars either side respectively, with Athenian ships standardizing on twenty-seven rowers (*thalamites*) on each side on the lower level. By this time the vessels were large enough to carry additional weaponry, for example artillery.

Ships of this design dominated the fleets Alexander used, and those he fought. However, as the Hellenistic period progressed larger polyremes began to appear as part of the wider successor arms race. These included *quadriremes*, *quinqueremes* (first used by the Syracusian dictator Dionysius 1 in 399 BC), *hexaremes*, *septiremes*, *octeres*, *enneres* and *deceres*. Demetrius and Ptolemy IV built even larger ships, the latter apparently a 'forty'. Such enormous vessels served principally as flagships, and platforms for heavy artillery. These larger polyremes derived their names not from the number of banks of oars but from the number of men rowing on each, over and above the third bank of the *trireme*. In this context, a quinquereme, or 'five', would feature a *trireme* arrangement but with two oarsmen rowing the top two tiers of oars, and one the bottom.

Classical and Hellenistic Greek war galleys also came with various degrees of protection. These were the 'aphract' (with the oarsmen unprotected by deck planking, as with the Athenian-led fleet that defeated the Persians at the Battle of Salamis in 480 BC), 'semi-cataphract' (oarsmen partially protected) and 'cataphract' (oarsmen fully protected). The larger line of battle ships in the Hellenistic period were usually of the cataphract type.

Chapter 2

Greece, Philip II, and Alexander

The world of Demetrius and the Antigonids was shaped by later Classical Greece, the rise of Macedon under Philip II and the mighty conquests of Alexander. Here I first detail the geography and language of the Greek world at the time to set the scene for all that follows. Next, I chronicle the rise of Macedonian hegemony over the Greek world, especially the role played by Philip II. This is important given it introduces the Antigonids, includes the birth of Demetrius, and narrates his early life. It also shows how these mighty Argead leaders proved such addictive role models for Demetrius' own later ambitions. The Macedonians always fêted the Olympian pantheon, especially Zeus and Hercules. To these Demetrius could now add two real-life heroes, Philip II and Alexander. Finally, I briefly detail Alexander's world-changing *anabasis*. This ends with his death in Babylon in the summer of 323 BC, the event which sparked the Wars of the Diadochi. Within a decade Antigonus and Demetrius were dominating the Hellenistic world.

Geography

The *poleis* of Classical Greece, and the regions under their control, formed a patchwork throughout the southern and central Balkans, the island chains of the Aegean Sea, and down the western coast of Anatolia. Greek colonies also thrived around the Black Sea, in Magna Graecia in southern Italy and Sicily, in Cyrene in modern Libya, and along the Mediterranean coasts of Gaul and Spain. Throughout this vast region there were over 1,000 city-states featuring many different systems of government, ranging from the two-king dictatorships of Sparta to Athens' occasional dalliance with democracy.

In the eastern Mediterranean, the key regions of the Greek world (running clockwise from the south) were:

- Crete.
- The Peloponnese, with Sparta in the south, Arcadia the centre, Elis the west, Achaea to its north and Argos to the east.
- The narrow Isthmus of Corinth and Attica. The former included Corinth, one of the 'fetters of Greece'. This was one of two cities which controlled access to key regions across the wider peninsula, the second being Chalcis. Demetrius himself added a third 'fetter' in Thessaly which he named after himself, Demetrias. Meanwhile Attica featured Athens, Laurion and Megara.
- To the north of the Peloponnese and Attica, Central Greece. In the east this featured the island of Euboea with its key cities of Oreos, Chalcis (see above) and Eretria. Moving westwards, we then have Boeotia and its key city of Thebes. To its north and west could be found Phocis with its key Temple of Apollo at Delphi, famed for its oracle. Finally, to the west could be found Lokris and Aetolia. The northern region of Central Greece is very mountainous and difficult to traverse for armies campaigning north to south, giving the resident Phocians and Aetolians much power there.
- To the northwest of the peninsula, Acarnania and Epirus. This region featured broad coastal plains that, heading east, soon rose to become the north-south Pindos Mountain range. Off the coast here were the key Ionian Sea island city-states of Zakynthos, Kephallenia and Corcyra (respectively modern Zante, Kefalonia and Corfu), traditionally with four others called the Heptanese.
- Across the Pindos Mountains and above eastern Central Greece, the broad plains of Thessaly, the key horse breeding region in the Balkans Peninsula. Here was also found Mount Olympus, home of the Olympian Gods.

- To the north of Thessaly, the Kingdom of Macedon and its royal cities of Aegae (modern Vergina) and Pella. The former was the original capital, and when later replaced by Pella became the kingdom's key religious centre and royal burial ground. At its southeastern tip sat the three-pronged Chalcidice Peninsula (today, the Halkidiki Peninsula), home to many Greek colonial cities, a region finally conquered by Philip II in 349 BC.
- Ranging above Macedonia, Illyria in the far northwest of the Balkans, then Paeonia to the east, and finally Thrace. All were famed in the classical world for their fierce warriors. Above Thrace, along the Black Sea coast, could then be found the many Greek colonies established there from the seventh century BC onwards. Key examples included Tomis (modern Constanta in Romania), Istria and Boristhenis (modern Odessa).
- Crossing into Anatolia, the Greek colonial cities running down the Ionian coast and its hinterland. These included some of the leading cultural centres in the entire Greek-speaking world, for example Pergamon, Ephesus, Prienne, Miletus and Halicarnassus.
- The various island chains of the Aegean Sea and beyond, including the large islands of Lesbos, Chios and Samos in the northern Aegean, the Sporades off Euboea, the islands in the Saronic Gulf south of Athens, the Cyclades in the south-central Aegean, and in the southeastern Aegean the Dodecanese featuring the large island *polis* of Rhodes, one of the Greek world's leading naval powers.

A key point to note here is how much the terrain of the Balkans Peninsula and Anatolia impacted armies campaigning there, with much activity taking place along the coast and its hinterland, and down the valleys of the major river systems. In particular, control of the 'fetters' proved vital. Additionally, the famous east-coast pass at Thermopylae in Central Greece was the scene of frequent conflict as the *poleis* in the Peloponnese and Attica strove to keep out northern invaders.

Language

Though the first speakers of proto-Greek were the Mycenaeans, it was the Dorian invasions from the northeastern Balkans from 1,150 BC that introduced the earliest form of true ancient Greek. The dialect they introduced soon replaced proto-Greek, with writing in ancient Greek appearing in the eighth century BC for the first time. This was through interaction with Phoenician traders in the Levant.

By the Classical Greek period ancient Greek had spread throughout the eastern Mediterranean and evolved into many different dialects, all still extant at the time of Philip II, Alexander and Demetrius. These included:

- The Western Group, featuring the oldest dialects, comprising –
  - Northwestern Greek, including (north to south) Epirus, Ambracia, Acarnania, and Phocis. This dialect was also spoken in the western Peloponnese, for example in Locris.
  - Doric, by this time spoken only in the southern and eastern Peloponnese, including the key city-states of Sparta, Argos and Corinth, and on Crete.
  - Achaean Doric, an antique form of the language spoken in the northern Peloponnese and the Ionian Sea islands.
- The Aeolic Group, comprising –
  - Aegean/Asiatic Aeolic, spoken on the northern Aegean Sea islands and along the northern Ionic coast of Anatolia.
  - Thessalian, spoken in Thessaly.
  - Boeotian, spoken in Boeotia in Central Greece.
- The Ionic-Attic Group, comprising –
  - Attic, spoken in Attica and in the colonies of Athens in the northern Aegean, including the islands of Skyros and Lemnos.
  - Ionic, spoken around the Aegean. This sub-dialect was broken down into three specific groups:
    - Euboean, also spoken in the Chalcidice Peninsula and in many of the colonies of Magna Graecia in Italy and Sicily.

        - Cycladic, spoken among the islands in the southern Aegean.
        - Asiatic Ionic, spoken in the *poleis* along the southwestern Anatolian coast and its hinterland.
- The Arcadocypriot Group, the most primitive of the ancient Greek language groups, comprising –
    - Arcadian, spoken in the mountainous interior of the Peloponnese. This dialect retained strong links with the earlier proto-Greek spoken by the Mycenaeans and may have been a direct descendent.
    - Cypriot, very similar to Arcadian with additional influences from the various language groups in the Levant given the Cypriot maritime trading network in the eastern Mediterranean.
- Ancient Macedonian, this either a northern dialect of ancient Greek (with strong Euboean influences given the kingdom's proximity to the Chalcidice Peninsula), or less likely a separate Hellenic language. This dialect gradually fell out of use in elite circles in Macedon in the early fourth century BC through interaction with Athens, and by the time of Philip II, Alexander and Demetrius Attic Greek was the dominant dialect there. This proved a hugely important development as it formed the basis of Koine Greek, the *lingua franca* of the Hellenistic world following the conquests of Alexander.

The Rise of Macedon

Macedon was regarded as an uncouth northern outsider in mainland Greece, with its mixed population of Macedonians, Illyrians and Thracians.[1] While the city-states to the south had found fame, fortune or tragedy through the various Persian invasions of Greece and the lengthy Peloponnesian War, Macedon stayed a place of difference, excluded from Greek affairs. At best, the *poleis* thought it a useful buffer to keep the uncouth 'barbarians' in the far north out of 'civilized' Central Greece, Attica and the Peloponnese. As Green details, 'southern Greeks never lost an opportunity of sneering at Macedonian 'barbarism'.[2]

The early kingdom was split into two natural parts, a lowland/ coastal region ruled by the Argead dynasty, and the highlands above reaching northwards to Paeonia. This upland zone featured tribal regions including Orestis, Lyncos and Elimaia, ruled by semi-independent dynasties that occasionally acknowledged the Argeads to their south as rulers. By the time of Philip II many of these highland kingdoms had been fully conquered by their more powerful lowland neighbour, a process he concluded. However, this did give the kingdom of Philip, Alexander and their Hellenistic successors a particular brittleness that continually required military success to maintain the authority of the monarch. Robin Lane Fox best describes this later kingdom of Macedon as:

> a broad patchwork of kingdoms, stitched together by conquest, marriage, and the bribes and attractions of Philip's rising fortunes.[3]

In Macedon proper, the Argeads had ruled unchallenged as kings since the seventh century BC when the dynasty had been founded. The Argead name gives a clue to its origins, the word deriving via the Latin *Argīvus* from the Greek Ἀργεῖος, meaning 'from Argos' in the eastern Peloponnese. Here, the Argead creation myth had a nobleman who claimed descent from Temenus, the great-great-grandson of the Olympian demi-God Hercules (himself the son of Zeus, head of the Olympian pantheon), setting out north from Argos to conquer a new kingdom which became Macedon. This link to Hercules and Zeus was heavily exploited by the Argeads, hence the local aristocracy rarely challenging the dynasty's hegemony. As Adrian Goldsworthy details, because of this illustrious heritage:

> only an Argead could be king of Macedon, a rule that was never broken until the final extinction of the line with the murder of Alexander IV, son of Alexander the Great, in 310 BC. Something in the Argead bloodline was seen as so special and sacred that the king had an important role as somehow more closely connected to the Gods.[4]

This link to the Olympian pantheon, later exploited to extremes by Demetrius, was writ through every aspect of Macedonian kingship. For example, every Royal day began with the king personally sacrificing a beast by slitting its throat, wherever he was resident, even in the field. To that end, it was also the king's religious as well as royal duty to lead his army on campaign and in battle from the front. Given that the kingdom was beset by potential enemies on all sides, with Epirots to the west, Illyrians and Paeonians to the north, Thracians to the east and the Greek *poleis* to the south, there was never a shortage of opportunity to do so.

Such Argead dominance of elite rule in Macedon should have seen political stability quickly settle in northern Greece, but this proved not to be the case. This was because there was a simple flaw in the system of Argead hegemony, namely the size of the wider royal family. To that end, any male member of the Argead line could make a bid for power if they had enough support from the wider nobility and population. Although it was usual for an elder son, if of age and capable, to succeed his father to the throne, there was no legal requirement that this should take place. Indeed, given the Argead tradition of polygamy, there was never a lack of candidates for the throne given the profusion of their offspring, hence the sense of jeopardy when Alexander succeeded his father Phillip. The candidate simply had to put himself before his Macedonian subjects high and low, most often in the form of the nobility and army, to gain their acclamation. If he succeeded he became king. If he failed, he would die well before his time.

This is precisely how Philip became king. In 364 BC he had returned to Macedon after his time in exile as a young man in Thebes. However, in 359 BC his brother Perdiccas III died in battle fighting the Illyrians, leaving his infant son Amyntas IV to succeed him as king. Given the child's age, Perdiccas had decreed before heading north that if he died

Philip would become regent. However, he soon usurped his young nephew with the support of the army, becoming Philip II.

The new king was immediately in action, fighting off a Paeonian invasion to the north before turning his attention to the Illyrians who had killed his elder brother. These were also defeated in short order, with any independent highland regions now formally bought under Macedonian hegemony. His swift military success cemented him firmly in power, with his newly won reputation as a young, dynamic military leader soon spreading throughout Greece. A period of political and financial stability followed in Macedon, with any potential rivals to the throne quickly eliminated.

Philip's real skill as a political leader now came to the fore. The kingdom's principal source of wealth was gold and silver mining, which he secured through territorial expansion. He then introduced the latest technological innovations through the recruitment of the finest mining and metallurgy experts from across Greece to help increase output. Meanwhile, the ever-inquisitive king also sought advice on how to increase agricultural output. The increased revenue from mining and farming then enabled Philip to initiate the reform for which he is best known, modernizing the Macedonian army (see Chapter 1).

Philip next turned to domestic matters, marrying the first of his seven wives in early 358 BC, before heading out on campaign once more. First he targeted the Illyrians again, inflicting a crushing defeat using his new *sarissa*-armed pike phalanx and companion cavalry. Taking another wife, he then turned his attention to the Greek *poleis* to the south, forming an alliance with the Chalcidian League to counter the growing hostility of Athens. He then took his army south into Thessaly, securing the support of the city-states there through two more marriages.

However, it was Philip's fifth marriage in later 357 BC that became his most important. This was to Olympias, daughter of the late Molossian king Neoptolemus I and future mother of Alexander the Great. It is because of his remarkable later exploits that we know more about his mother than any of Philip's other wives, or indeed any other woman at the Macedonian court.

By this time the growing size of Philip's military establishment was outstripping his finances. Soon he was casting around for a cause that would allow him to intervene in Central Greece, Attica and the Peloponnese where loot could be found. He found one in the Sacred War. This broke out in 356 BC when the Phocians shocked the wider Greek world by seizing the Temple of Apollo in Delphi, and its fabulous treasure. This was just the sort of cause Philip had been looking for, and in 353 BC he invaded Thessaly. There he defeated a marauding army of 7,000 Phocian mercenaries. When the Phocians mounted a counter offensive Philip crushed them at the Battle of Crocus Field in late 353 BC, killing over 6,000 and enslaving 3,000 more.

Philip's success here earned him immense prestige among the Greek *poleis* given that he was representing a common cause. Thessaly now fell under Macedonian hegemony. Then in 349 BC he targeted the final independent Greek colony on the Chalcidice Peninsula, Olynthus. Here Athens had invested much diplomatic and financial capital in convincing its rulers to remain independent. To Philip that was a challenge he couldn't ignore, and he began an extensive siege that saw Olynthus fall a year later to his new siege machinery. The city was razed to the ground.

However, in late 347 BC Philip was dragged back to the Sacred War, still rumbling on to the south. The Phocians were still causing trouble and at the request of Thebes and Boeotia Philip gathered his army and marched south again. Both Athens and Sparta reacted with alarm, horrified at the prospect of Philip's ultra-modern army campaigning in Greece proper. The former voted to raise a force of citizen hoplites and sent a squadron of *trireme* war galleys to patrol the Thessalian coast, while the latter sent 1,000 elite hoplites and supporting troops to block the pass at Thermopylae. Events soon overtook the Greek allies though. A change of leadership in Phocis saw the war end, with Philip signing a peace agreement with Athens and Sparta called the Treaty of Philocrates, named after the chief Athenian negotiator.

With relations with his Greek rivals reset for now, Philip received Athenian and other Greek delegations to the Macedonian capital Pella in 346 BC. While there he had time to visit his children by his various wives. This included the young Alexander, who was now ten years old and clearly the heir apparent. True to his nature, Philip spared no expense in his education, later famously recruiting Aristotle to become Alexander's tutor as he grew to early manhood. Philip also surrounded him with a group of other young men from leading Macedonian families who would accompany him for much of his later life. It is also around this time we have the famous story of Alexander taming the headstrong charger Bucephalas in front of his father and the king's companions. This is one of the most famous anecdotes about Alexander, with Plutarch saying that on seeing Alexander's bravery with the headstrong horse Philip said, probably apocryphally:

> My boy, you must find a kingdom big enough for your ambitions. Macedon is too small for you.[5]

However, Philip's attention was soon drawn south again where friction with Athens was once more growing after a change in leadership there. In 340 BC war broke out between the two. Rather than target Attica directly, Philip again headed east, this time to campaign against the Athenian colonies along the Sea of Marmara. This coincided with Alexander's coming of age, and when Philip set off to war the boy was left in charge in Pella to rule as regent. Alexander quickly had the chance to test his skills in battle as, in Philip's absence, the Thracian

Maedi tribe rebelled against Macedonian rule. Alexander, no doubt well guided by the council of nobles appointed by the king to advise him, responded swiftly, defeating them in his first victory.

In 339 BC Philip looked south again, where Thebes had chosen to side with Athens. He marched there in the late Autumn of 339 BC, cleverly wrong-footing the Thebans by ignoring the pass at Thermopylae. Instead, he headed through mountainous Central Greece, swiftly capturing Cytinium near the high Gravia Pass above Amphissa. With this route open, he then descended onto the border of northern Boeotia where he occupied the city of Elatea. Here he was well placed to command the lowland access points through Central Greece into Attica, and onwards to the Peloponnese. The king now consolidated, awaiting a large contingent of Thessalian allies who promptly arrived in good order. He was also joined by Alexander.

With Philip now poised above Attica like the sword of Damocles, panic gripped Athens, with magistrates hurriedly leaving their dinner tables to set up an emergency meeting. Here the Athenian statesman Demosthenes convinced those eligible to vote to seek a formal alliance with Thebes to fight Philip. Both Athens and the king then sent embassies to win the Boeotian city's favour. Athens emerged the winner.

Philip now deployed a stratagem to wrong-foot his enemies, making it known he planned to head back north to deal with a rebellion in Thrace. He then led some of his army back towards the Gravia Pass to give the impression he was heading north. However, in the dead of night he then doubled the troops back south where, joined by the rest of his army, he swiftly occupied Amphissa. From this position he could threaten the lines of supply of the combined armies of the Athenians, Thebans and their allies who by now were gathering in northern Boeotia. They quickly withdrew out of Philip's immediate reach, setting up a new camp near the Boeotian city of Chaeronea. Both sides now paused for breath, with Philip sending envoys to Athens and Thebes to ask for peace. However, in Athens Demosthenes was in no mood to do a deal and again his oratory won the day in rejecting the Macedonian offer. This stiffened the resolve of the Thebans too.

Battle was now inevitable and at the beginning of August Philip again moved on the allies. Soon the two armies were camped a few kilometres apart near Chaeronea, where battle was finally joined on 2 August. The result was a spectacular victory for Philip and Alexander, the *sarissa*-armed phalanx pinning the enemy in place while the shock cavalry led by Alexander broke the hoplite line. A massacre ensued. Diodorus Siculus provides detail here, saying:

> Alexander, anxious to give his father proof of his valour ... was the first to break through the main body of the enemy directly opposing him, slaying many; and bore down all before him – and his men, pressing on closely, cut to pieces the lines of the enemy; and after the ground had been piled with the dead, put the wing resisting him to flight.[6]

Philip's victory at Chaeronea was total, with any Greek opposition shattered. The king and Alexander now marched unopposed through southern Boeotia into Attica and then on to the Peloponnese. By this time the ever-ambitious Philip had his eyes on an even greater prize, namely Achaemenid Persia, mainland Greece's traditional enemy. He therefore needed to leave a stable Greece to his rear before he looked eastwards. This meant first dealing with his opponents at Chaeronea, and then winning over the other city-states in southern Greece.

First, he marched on Thebes which immediately surrendered, its leaders expecting the worst. However, instead of sacking the city that had been his home when he was a hostage there, he simply expelled those Theban leaders who'd opposed him, recalling any exiled pro-Macedonian leaders and installing a Macedonian garrison. He treated Athens even more leniently.

Next, Philip gathered the great and the good from across southern Greece at Corinth, where in 337 BC he established his League of Corinth, modelled on the old anti-Achaemenid Persian alliance dating back to the Greco-Persian wars, with the members agreeing never to wage war against each other unless to suppress a revolt. The alliance included all of the leading city-states in Central Greece, Attica and the Peloponnese except Sparta, which remained aloof from Philip's now-otherwise-unchallenged Macedonian hegemony in Greece. The king was soon declared the *hegemon* (supreme leader) of all Greece, and quickly turned his attention to the one subject he knew could unify all the Greeks, his planned war with Persia.

Ever the careful planner, Philip knew his enemy well and moved quickly once his new league was in place. In early 336 BC he appointed Parmenion, his most experienced *strategos,* to command an initial invasion force with orders to cross the Hellespont into Persian-controlled Anatolia. Comprising 10,000 veterans, the force landed in Asia where it met minimal Persian resistance. Soon many of the Greek Ionian cities along the western Anatolian coast rebelled against Persian rule, throwing out the trappings of satrapal rule and welcoming the Macedonians as their saviours. However, back in Macedon, events suddenly took a dramatic turn for the worse.

When Philip returned to Pella he fell in love with Cleopatra Eurydice, niece of his general Attalus. They married soon after, the event making Alexander feel less secure given if Philip and Cleopatra had a male child the boy might become the preferred candidate as the next king. His insecurity was on full display when the wedding took place, the event ending disastrously for both Philip and Alexander. Plutarch provides the detail, saying:

> At the wedding of Cleopatra and Philip, she being much too young for him, her uncle Attalus in his drink desired the Macedonians would

> implore the gods to give them a lawful successor to the kingdom by his niece [Olympias being Epirot]. This so irritated Alexander, that throwing one of the cups at his head, 'You villain,' said he, 'What, am I then a bastard?' Then Philip, taking Attalus' part, rose up and would have run his son through; but by good fortune for them both, either his over-hasty rage, or the wine he had drunk, made his foot slip, so that he fell down on the floor. At which Alexander reproachfully insulted him: 'See there,' said he, '...the man who makes preparations to pass out of Europe into Asia, overturned in passing from one seat to another.'[7]

The heir now fled west with Olympias and his close friends. He left his mother in the safe hands of her brother Alexander I, by now king of Epirus. Alexander then escaped northwest to Illyria where he sought refuge. Here he and his entourage were treated as honoured guests. However, given the years Philip had spent grooming Alexander for the throne, and his genuine affection for his son, it seems unlikely that Philip ever intended to severely punish him, let alone remove him as heir. Accordingly, Alexander soon returned to Macedon after a six-month self-imposed exile.

However, for Philip disaster loomed. In October 336 BC, at the same time Parmenion was winning Ionian Greek hearts and minds, the great and the good from all over Greece gathered in Aegae to celebrate the wedding of Olympias' brother Alexander I with Alexander's full-sister (and Alexander I's own niece) Cleopatra. As part of the celebrations the 46-year-old Philip entered the town's theatre at the culmination of a procession of twelve statues of the key Olympian Gods, and one of himself. Philip was unarmed, wearing a simple tunic bleached pure white. He had no close-protection with him, the king's seven personal bodyguards ringing the arena at a distance. As he reached the centre of the arena, one of them suddenly ran towards him before anyone else could react. This was Pausanias of Orestis, a young man recently promoted to the post as recompense for very rough treatment (which may have included rape) at the hands of Philip's now father-in-law Attalus and his cronies. Pausanias, also a lover of Philip when a youth, felt Attalus hadn't been punished enough for his abuse. From that point, even as a close royal guard, he nursed a sense of grievance against the king. This was certainly encouraged by those in court who were set against Attalus, including Alexander and Olympias. Now, as Pausanias reached the king, he dropped his ceremonial javelin and drew a long dagger hidden beneath his cloak. He struck immediately, stabbing Philip viciously between the ribs before anyone could react. The *hegemon* of all Greece, set to lead the Greeks on their crusade against the Persians, died within seconds, bleeding into the sand of the arena.

After a shocked silence pandemonium broke out. The assassin immediately tried to escape, racing towards associates waiting for him with horses near the arena entrance. However, closely pursued by three fellow guards, he tripped on a vine root and was quickly killed with javelins, his corpse subsequently crucified.

Matters moved quickly from that point. Antipater, the leading Macedonian noble with Parmenion away, quickly presented Alexander to an assembly of the nobility and army as Philip's successor. Given the kingdom's many foreign policy commitments, all knew the last thing Macedon needed at that point was a contested Argead succession. The massed gathering swiftly acclaimed Philip's second legitimate son as Alexander III of Macedon.

Next, at a hastily convened assembly of the League of Corinth, Alexander replaced his father as the *hegemon* in charge of the planned Greek campaign against the Persians. The new king then returned north to campaign against the Illyrians and Thracians to secure his borders, before again heading south when false rumours of his death prompted Thebes, urged on by Athens, to revolt against Macedonian rule. Alexander arrived after a forced march, sacked the city and razed it to the ground. Over 6,000 Thebans lost their lives, with the rest of the population sold into slavery. The destruction of Thebes cowed any further insurrection in Greece. However, from that point, a deep sense of distrust existed between the Macedonians and Greeks, verging on enmity in the case of Athens and Sparta. Alexander then left garrisons in Corinth, Chalcis and the Cadmea citadel of Thebes (which he had left still standing) before finally turning his attention to his father's planned Persian expedition.

The Antigonids

Amid the triumphs and drama of Philip II's rise to hegemony over the Greek world, the future Antigonid dynasty emerged onto the historical stage. Here I provide pen portraits of its founder, Antigonus Monophthalmus, and his son Demetrius, to set the scene for their fantastical later exploits across the Hellenistic world.

Antigonus was born in 382 BC, the same year as Philip II. Little is known of his early life save his father was called Philip (this based on an inscription found in Priene, Ionia, dated to 334 BC), with Aelian claiming he was of a labourer of humble origins.[8] Philip seems to have died young after fathering two other sons called Ptolemy and Demetrius. Antigonus' mother then married a second time, having another son called Marsyas who was later one of the young Alexander's school mates. This gives the lie to Aelian's suggestion of Antigonus' humble birth, the family most likely lowland Macedonian aristocracy. Justin says Antigonus was a companion to both Philip II and Alexander, and later a key member of Alexander's inner circle.[9]

Antigonus' early career in the Macedonian army was unremarkable, his progress through the senior ranks steady. In Philip's early campaigns he commanded units of the phalanx, with Plutarch detailing a Macedonian leader called Antigonus who lost an eye to a catapult bolt at the Siege of Perinthus in 340 BC.[10] This is most likely our

Antigonus. Later, after Philip's murder, Antigonus was placed in charge of Alexander's non-Macedonian troops, particularly the Greek hoplites. He then fought at the Battle of the Granicus in 334 BC, alongside his younger brother Ptolemy.

However, Antigonus did not accompany Alexander on his *anabasis*. Instead, he was appointed the new Macedonian governor of Phrygia after Alexander conquered it. This was a key region in central Anatolia, notable for Alexander's knot-defeating exploits in Gordium, its former capital. More importantly, it sat astride the main land route through central Anatolia to the Balkans. It was therefore vital to the success of Alexander's eastern expansion, protecting the key logistics route between the frontline and home.

Antigonus was soon in action, winning three battles against Persian remnant armies, leading 1,500 Greek hoplites Alexander had left him. He then campaigned with his neighbouring governors Asander in Lydia and Calasa in Hellespontine Phrygia, expanding conquered Macedonian territory throughout the region.

Once secure in post, Antigonus established Celaenae as his regional capital. The city was well known to the Greeks as the place where Xenophon had mustered his Greek mercenaries when fighting for Cyrus the Younger in 401 BC. He gives a fine description, saying:

> It is a populous city of Phrygia, large and rich. Here Cyrus owned a palace and a large park full of wild beasts, which he used to hunt on horseback, whenever he wished to give himself or his horses exercise. Through the midst of the park flows the River Maeander, the sources of which are within the palace buildings, and it flows through the city. The great king also has another palace in Celaenae, a strong place, on the sources of another river, the Marsyas, at the foot of the acropolis. This river also flows through the city, discharging itself into the Maeander, and is five-and-twenty feet broad. Here is the place where Apollo is said to have flayed Marsyas, when he had conquered him in the contest of

> skill. He hung up the skin of the conquered man in the cavern where the spring wells forth, hence the name of the river, Marsyas.[11]

Quintus Curtius Rufus provides further detail, adding:

> It was well known for its enormous park and the great fortified tetrapyrgia estates immediately around the town which evince the richness of the agriculture and husbandry of a countryside abounding in wealthy villages.[12]

All in all, very much the kind of place for a new governor to set up shop.

We have our first physical descriptions of Antigonus from this time. Contemporary writers call him a giant of a man, big and burly with a booming voice, and with immense physical and mental energy. One who had bided his time while Alexander's younger commanders grabbed the headlines of conquest. But a man who knew how to make the most of an opportunity. Which he duly did, for there was no other Macedonian better placed to control access to the Macedonian east when Alexander died in Babylon in the summer of 323 BC.

Demetrius was the eldest son of Antigonus and his wife Stratonice, the daughter of another leading Macedonian noble, Coragus. The latter, one of Alexander's close bodyguards, would later find infamy while campaigning with Alexander in Asia due to his inferior wrestling skills. Here, Diodorus Siculus takes up the story in 325 BC with the king back on his feet after a near fatal arrow wound while campaigning in the east. I record it in full given Coragus was Demetrius' grandfather, and the event an important part of later Antigonid folklore. The Greek historian says:

> In the course of the drinking to celebrate the king's recovery a curious event occurred which is worth mention. Among the king's companions there was his guard Coragus, strong in body, who had distinguished

> himself many times in battle. His temper was sharpened by the drink, and he challenged to single combat Dioxippus the Athenian, an athlete who had won a crown for boxing in the Olympic Games in 336 BC. As you would expect, the guests at the banquet egged them on and Dioxippus accepted. The king set a day for the contest, and when the time came, many myriads of men gathered to see the spectacle. The Macedonians and Alexander backed Coragus because he was one of them, while the Greeks backed Dioxippus. The two advanced to the field of honour, the Macedonian clad in his expensive armour but the Athenian naked, his body oiled, carrying a well-balanced club. Both men were fine to look upon with their magnificent physiques and their ardour for combat. Everyone looked forward, as it were, to a battle of gods. By his carriage and the brilliance of his arms, the Macedonian inspired terror as if he were Ares, while Dioxippus excelled in sheer strength and condition; still more because with his club he bore a certain resemblance to Hercules. As they approached each other, the Macedonian flung his javelin from a proper distance, but the other inclined his body slightly and avoided its impact. Then the Macedonian poised his long spear and charged, but the Greek, when he came within reach, struck it with his club and shattered it. After these two defeats, Coragus was reduced to continuing the battle with his sword, but as he reached for it, the other leaped upon him and seized his sword hand with his left, while with his right hand the Greek upset the Macedonian's balance and made him lose his footing. As he fell to the earth, Dioxippus placed his foot upon his neck and, holding his club aloft, looked to the spectators. The crowd was in an uproar because of the stunning quickness and superiority of the man's skill, and the king signed to let Coragus go, then broke up the gathering and left. He was plainly annoyed at the defeat of the Macedonian.[13]

Here we see a master of pankration at work, the ancient Greek art of unarmed combat. It did Dioxippus little good though. He later committed suicide after being unfairly accused of theft by disgruntled Macedonians angry at his victory over Coragus.

Demetrius was born in Pella in 337 BC. He was named after his father's younger brother and had a younger brother himself called Philip. We have no detail of whether Antigonus took more than one wife, though this would have been normal for a Macedonian nobleman, and if so whether Demetrius had any half siblings. Plutarch adds some salacious gossip at this point, saying:

> Some have it that Demetrius was not the son, but the nephew of Antigonus; for his own father died when the boy was quite young, and then his mother immediately married Antigonus, so that Demetrius was considered to be his son.[14]

This is the only mention we have of this, and most modern commentators disregard it. I will too.

Sadly, tragedy soon struck the family, with Demetrius' brother Philip dying at a young age of causes unknown. Not so the elder boy though. He grew up bright, fit and strong, with contemporary writers noting his flawless good looks. Romm calls him a 'tall, athletic boy with exquisite features'.[15]

Demetrius remained at home in Pella when Antigonus set off for Asia in 334 BC. As he grew one can imagine his frustration as tales of the king's astonishing exploits arrived there with every despatch, describing fabulous far-off places few in the Macedonian capital had ever heard of. However, once Antigonus had settled into his new governorship in Celaenae he summoned his family to join him. This was likely in 330 BC. It was here, in the lush countryside around Celaenae and its governor's palace, that Demetrius grew to manhood. Plutarch, always a fan, tells a story showing how close he and his father were. The tale has the same apocryphal tone as that of Alexander meeting Persian ambassadors in Philip II's court in Pella when a boy. Plutarch says:

> Demetrius was also exceedingly fond of his father; and from his devotion to his mother it was apparent that he honoured his father also from genuine affection rather than out of deference to his power. On one occasion, when Antigonus was busy with an embassy, Demetrius came home from hunting; he went up to his father and kissed him, and then sat down by his side just as he was, javelins in hand. Then Antigonus, as the ambassadors were now going away with their answers, called out to them in a loud voice and said: 'O men, carry back this report also about us, that this is the way we feel towards one another,' implying his harmonious and trustful relations with his son.[16]

However, by his late teens, Demetrius was beginning to show a love of the high life which was to dog him for the rest of his life. Romm says:

> Like most adolescents, Demetrius was interested in sex, indeed more interested than most, in part because his good looks and family wealth gave him more opportunities. By the time of the Triparadeisos conclave he had already gained a reputation for philandering. In his family's palace at Celaenae, young women had come and gone from his bed in a manner that caused his father to wink at him knowingly with his one good eye.[17]

By the time of the Partition of Triparadeisos the Antigonids had actually left Celaenae, with the First War of the Diadochi well under way. However, it gives us a date as it took place in 320 BC. By that time Demetrius was 17 and already taking his place on the wider stage of the Hellenistic world fighting alongside his father. More of that later. For now, stepping back slightly in time, I briefly narrate the story of Alexander's conquests in Asia which set the scene for the Wars of the Diadochi after his death, and the rise and fall of the Antigonids.

Anabasis

In the annals of ancient history, the light of Alexander the Great shines brighter than any other, inspiring generations of dynasts and despots. Thus, we have Julius Caesar reduced to tears on seeing a statue of the Macedonian king when Caesar was himself the same age at which Alexander died. The experience left him feeling hopelessly diminished.

In true Argead fashion, Alexander was the embodiment of the Homeric warrior hero, always leading from the front with near suicidal courage. A regent at 16, cavalry commander at 18, king at 20 and conqueror of the biggest empire the world had ever known at 26. The explorer of mythical India at 30 where he reached the ends of his known earth, but wanted more. The man for whom achievable was never enough, and who later thought himself a god. And the man who set the bar very high indeed for one who, desperately by the end of his life, tried time and again to emulate his boyhood hero: Demetrius Poliorcetes.

At the time Alexander became king, all contemporary commentators describe his striking appearance. Plutarch for example says:

> Alexander possessed a number of individual features which many of his successors and friends later tried to reproduce, such as the poise of the neck which was tilted slightly to the left, or a certain melting look in the eyes.[18]

The reader will note this is exactly the way Demetrius chose to have himself portrayed in portraiture.

Though shorter in height than the average Macedonian man of the time, Alexander stood out among the older warriors at court by choosing to remain clean-shaven rather than grow the traditional beard (again, here he was emulated by Demetrius). He is described as having a fair complexion with a 'ruddy tinge', with tawny brown hair often likened to a lion's mane.[19] Notably, his eyes were also differently coloured through a condition called heterochromia iridium, with one brown and the other blue grey, giving him an unsettling stare that he used to great effect when needed. This disorder can be caused by trauma, either at birth or later in life, or very rarely by genetics.

Alexander was already an accomplished warrior when he became king. He soon turned his attention to his father's great project, the destruction of Achaemenid Persia. In the spring of 334 BC he launched his invasion and was swiftly joined by Parmenion's army, already in western Anatolia. He was accompanied by the cast of characters, some the same age and some older, who would go on to shape the future Hellenistic world. These included Ptolemy, Seleucus, Lysimachus, Eumenes, Antigonus Monophthalmus, Perdiccas, Craterus, Leonnatus and Peithon.

Alexander moved quickly once in Asia. Learning the local satrapal army was gathering to challenge him, he sought battle immediately. The key engagement occurred at the Granicus River in May 334 BC. Here Alexander won the first of his four mighty set-piece victories. (Given that this book is not his story, I have included detail of each in Appendix B.)

After his victory in western Anatolia Alexander quickly captured the regional capital Sardis, securing vast amounts of plunder. He then spent the next six months subduing any cities on the Ionian coast that had stayed loyal to Persia. Most surrendered immediately. Those that didn't were flattened. Then, after a brief diversion to central Phrygia where he unravelled the Gordian Knot by slashing it in half with his sword, he headed for Syria. Here he won his next set-piece victory against the Persians in 333 BC at Issus. This time Darius III was present with his royal army, but fled back to Persia when the battle turned against him.

Alexander chose not to pursue the Persian king, instead staying to subdue the Levantine coast given this controlled much of the trade in the eastern Mediterranean. Here the Macedonian king spent seven months besieging the key island city of Tyre, building a massive causeway to help capture this major fleet base and port. Similarly, he invested Gaza, before then entering Egypt. There he was welcomed as a liberator and crowned pharaoh, also founding the city which still carries his name to this day, Alexandria.

The Macedonian king now turned his attention back to Darius, returning to Tyre before launching a huge campaign down the Tigris valley. This eventually bought the Persian king to battle at Gaugamela near Erbil in modern Iraq in 331 BC. This was arguably Alexander's finest victory, with Darius fleeing eastwards once more.

With the Persian army smashed, Alexander then quickly captured the key Persian city of Babylon. Here for the first time he confirmed the sitting Achaemenid satrap (governor) would remain in place to govern his satrapy as part of the new Macedonian hierarchy. This was Mazaeus, his reappointment our first real indication of Alexander's emerging wider plan to incorporate aspects of the existing Persian administration into his post-conquest settlement across Darius' former empire. This is also the first point we see a schism developing between the pragmatic king and many in the ultra-conservative Macedonian high command, excepting his close circle of friends.

However, Alexander was a young man in a hurry. For him there would be no dawdling.

Soon he captured the Persian capital cities of Susa and Persepolis. The latter he burnt to the ground. In the summer of 330 BC he then set out again at high speed, heading northeast. Travelling via Rhagae near modern Tehran, he was soon through the Caspian Gates and into the Caucasus Mountains. There he learned that Bessus, Achaemenid satrap of Bactria, had deposed Darius. Later, as the Macedonians closed on the new Persian king near Shāhrūd in northeastern Iran, they learned that Bessus had killed Darius. Alexander, shocked, sent the body back to Persepolis for burial with all due honours in the royal tombs there.

Alexander consolidated briefly to ensure his lines of supply were secure (note the key role played by Antigonus in Phrygia here), and then set off eastwards once more in 327 BC. Crossing the Elburz Mountains in northern Iran he arrived at the Hyrcanian Ocean, today's Caspian Sea. He seized Zadracarta in Hyrcania where he received the submission of the remaining Achaemenid Persian satraps and nobles. Here he re-confirmed the most capable in their offices, following the example of Mazaeus in Babylon.

The king then briefly turned westwards to modern Amol, reducing a mountain people there called the Mardi in the Elburz Mountains. Here he also accepted the surrender of the last Greek mercenaries who had been in Persian employ. Alexander continued east, advancing rapidly again and crossing into modern Afghanistan where he founded Alexandria in Ariana near modern Herat.

However, disaster then struck at Phrada in Drangiana. Here the king discovered a plot to assassinate him. Worse, Parmenion's son Philotas, who by now commanded the companion cavalry, was implicated. He was tried and condemned by the army, and then executed. Alexander knew that Parmenion would seek revenge for his son's death and sent a secret message to Cleander, Parmenion's second in command back in Media. This ordered him to assassinate his superior, which Cleander duly did.[20] All Parmenion's close colleagues were also quietly dispatched.

Given Parmenion's high standing, these actions caused widespread horror among the Macedonians. However, they also strengthened Alexander's position with the older officers who had served under Philip as their cards had now been marked. Their earlier dissatisfaction at the reappointment of Mazaeus in Babylon had been noted. From now on, anyone who crossed the king knew that, no matter how senior they were, a miserable end was the likely outcome.

From Phrada, Alexander next marched even further east. Advancing up the valley of the Helmand River through Arachosia, he passed the site of modern Kabul. The king then entered the territory of the Paropamisadae, where he founded Alexandria by the Caucasus. Bessus, murderer of Darius, was now in Bactria trying to raise a revolt in the eastern satrapies. Taking the title Great King, he styled himself Artaxerxes V. Alexander acted with his usual efficiency, crossing the Hindu Kush via the 3,850 m high Khawak Pass and then heading north with his full field army. Despite bitter cold and food shortages, the army soon arrived at Drapsaca in Afghanistan north of Kabul. Bessus, outflanked, fled again. He crossed the River Oxus heading back west, with Alexander in hot pursuit after appointing loyal satraps in Bactria and Aria to secure his rear. By the time Alexander neared the fugitive again, the Sogdian warlord Spitamenes had deposed him. Captured and flogged, Bessus was handed to the Macedonians and then sent back to Bactria. There he was mutilated in the Persian manner, losing his nose and ears, and was then publicly executed at Ecbatana in western Persia.[21]

Alexander now turned north again, reaching Maracanda (modern Samarkand) by way of Cyropolis. In short order he reached the River Jaxartes, the modern Syr Darya River, which was the most northerly border of the former Persian Empire. Here he fought and won the Battle of the Jaxartes against local Scythian nomads. The site of this campaign straddles the borders of modern Tajikistan, Uzbekistan, Kyrgyzstan and Kazakhstan, lying southwest of Tashkent (the modern capital of Uzbekistan). Alexander then pursued the defeated Scythians northwards into Central Asia. Dispersing them, he then returned south to the Jaxartes. Here he founded Alexandria Eschate (meaning 'the farthest') on the south bank at the site of the modern city of Khodjend in Tajikistan. The king then returned to Maracanda.

There, another incident occurred which radically widened the schism between Alexander and the Macedonians, particularly those of Philip's generation. This was the murder of his key general Cleitus the Black in a drunken quarrel. Arrian says in his detailed account of the incident that the actual cause of the feud was unknown, though Plutarch lays some of the blame with Cleitus for taking advantage of the king's anger and intoxication.[22] Others have argued more recently that Cleitus took offence at the older officers being insulted by the king's supporters. It seems Cleitus accused Alexander of taking personal credit for the feats of all the Macedonians, including previously his father. The result was fatal, Alexander impaling him with a pike. The king was full of remorse after the event. However, the damage had been done, with the split between Alexander and many of his troops widening. This was further manifest when Alexander started wearing Persian royal dress, a very visible expression of an eastern absolutist form of rule his opponents accused him of adopting. Shortly afterwards, the king tried to impose a Persian court ceremonial routine which involved *proscynesis*, a form of prostration. Normal for Persians when entering the king's presence, it implied an act of worship. The Macedonians and Greeks refused point-blank, even his most loyal supporters. In the short term at least, Alexander's multi-cultural experiment was put on hold.

Another plot against the king was soon uncovered which involved the royal pages.

Callisthenes, Alexander's historian and Aristotle's great nephew, was also implicated. Tried and convicted, he either died of disease in captivity or was tortured on the rack and hanged, with the other implicated pages stoned to death.[23] Relations between the king and his men worsened yet again.

Alexander now targeted India to the south. He left Bactria in the summer of 327 BC with the whole field army after capturing the Sogdian Rock fortress, leaving behind garrisons to secure his rear.

He re-crossed the Hindu Kush through Bamiyan and the Ghorband Valley and then divided his forces into two columns. The generals Hephaestion and Perdiccas took charge of half of the army and the baggage train, heading through the Khyber Pass. The king himself led the remainder south. As they cleared the foothills of the Himalayas they now saw spread out before them the broad forested expanse of the Punjab. Fabulous India beckoned, one more stop on Alexander's road to destiny and greatness.

Alexander's assault on India began with an advance through Swāt and Gandhara, deploying his force in multiple columns with the spearheads again led by Hephaestion and Perdiccas. Following the strategy detailed above, he gradually fought his way south and east through the Punjab, fighting multiple small-scale engagements on the way, mostly short sieges of regional fortified towns and citadels. The Macedonian king continued to lead from the front when needed, and in the winter of 327 BC was wounded fighting the Aspasioi in the Kunar Valley by a dart striking his shoulder and penetrating his linen armour, though he soon recovered.

Eventually Alexander forced a route to the Indus, and then stormed the supposedly impregnable pinnacle of Aornos (modern Pir-Sar). This was within a day's march of the Indus itself, which he crossed in the spring of 326 BC near Attock, the army then entering Taxila. Here the ruler, Taxiles (also called Ambhi), gave the king elephants and Indian troops in return for his support against his rival Porus. This was the context for Alexander's last great set-piece victory, fought on the left bank of the Hydaspes River, which I detail in Appendix B.

Alexander continued to campaign in the region, founding two new cities called Alexandria Nicaea and Bucephala, the latter named after his horse Bucephalus who died there. After founding the latter, Alexander sacrificed to the sun, showing his determination to continue ever eastwards on his *anabasis*. Then fighting his way further into the

Punjab, he soon reached the River Hyphasis (the modern Beas River) in late August 326 BC. However, here his exhausted and homesick army finally mutinied in the tropical rain, refusing to go any further. Alexander made a determined effort to change their minds, using fine oratory and calling specifically on the honour and reputation of his senior leaders, but finally he had to accept the inevitable. The king then erected twelve altars to the Olympian Gods, and built a fort he named Alexandria Hyphasis on the western bank of the river near modern Amritsar. This last was an interesting initiative, Alexander perhaps hoping he would one day return east and resume his *anabasis*. However, for now he realized that dream was over.

After fighting his way to the coast, Alexander constructed a new stone-built harbour and dockyard, and then divided his army again for the journey home. One column, under Craterus, was sent through the Mulla Pass, Quetta and Kandahar into the Helmand Valley, and then onwards to Drangiana with the aim of re-joining other elements of the main army on the Amanis River in Carmania in south-eastern Iran. This force included the baggage train, three battalions of the phalanx, the king's newly acquired elephants and the sick and wounded. Meanwhile another force, under the Cretan admiral Nearchus, set sail in September 325 BC in 150 ships for the Persian Gulf. Alexander himself led the rest of the foot soldiers along the coast through Gedrosia (modern Baluchistan in south-western Pakistan). Some argue that Alexander actually planned for Nearchus' fleet to supply this column, but it may have sailed too late due to the prevailing winds. In any event, the land force was soon forced inland away from the coast by the mountainous terrain, and the march west through the Gedrosian Desert became a disaster due to the serious shortage of food and water. Additionally, many of the camp followers in the column died in a sudden monsoon that flooded their encampment in a wadi. Finally, after much suffering, the survivors re-joined Nearchus and the fleet on the Amanis.

Alexander was back in Susa in western Iran by the spring of 324 BC. There he made his boldest gesture to date regarding his desire to see the fusing of Macedonian and Persian culture. This was the mass wedding of himself and eighty of his senior officers to Persian wives in the context of a feast to celebrate his conquest of the Persian Empire. Alexander certainly set a precedent here, taking not one but two new wives, these being Darius III's eldest daughter Stateira, and Parysatis, youngest daughter of the earlier Persian king Artaxerxes III. At the same time, 10,000 of his line soldiers with native wives were given substantial dowries. Yet despite this generosity, his policy of racial fusion continued to go down badly with the Macedonians. Most had no sympathy for his concept of a cosmopolitan empire. In particular, his determination to add even more Persians into the army on an equal basis was bitterly resented. He pressed on with the plan anyway. Only Peucestas, the new governor of Persia, gave the policy his full support. However, most Macedonians viewed it as a direct threat to their own privileged position.

Things came to a head later that year in the ancient Babylonian city of Opis on the Tigris. Here Alexander announced his plan to send home, under the veteran phalanx leader Craterus, 10,000 of the oldest or least-fit phalangites. This was a sensible plan but it caused uproar among the Macedonians, who mutinied again. Alexander reacted with fury, with Arrian having him quicker to anger as he grew older.[24] The king arrested the thirteen ringleaders there and then, pointing them out personally. He then withdrew from all contact with the army and began substituting even more Persians for Macedonians, also giving Macedonian military titles to Persian units. The army was aghast, and the mutiny collapsed. An emotional scene of reconciliation followed outside the royal quarters, after which a vast banquet with 9,000 guests was held to celebrate the ending of the 'misunderstanding'. The

10,000 veterans were then sent back to Macedonia with gifts, and the crisis abated.

Alexander next tackled the problem of the thousands of mercenaries wandering throughout the empire. Many of those from the Greek-speaking world who had accompanied the Macedonians at the beginning of the *anabasis* were political exiles from their own cities. He therefore sent the 'Exiles Decree' to be read at the Olympic Games in September 324 BC. This required the Greek cities of the League of Corinth to receive back all exiles and their families. He also indicated at this point his desire to replace Antipater as regent back in Pella with the returning Craterus, viewing the latter as a more-loyal supporter than Philip's old friend.

Afterwards, Alexander moved on to Ecbatana, where he retrieved the bulk of the Achaemenid Persian imperial treasure. This was a mind-numbing amount of money, the wealth so vast it came to dominate Mediterranean politics for centuries, well into the Roman period.

Sadly for Alexander, while there his closest friend Hephaestion died. This devastated the Macedonian king. Deep in mourning, he then returned to Babylon where he began planning a new series of campaigns, including an invasion of Arabia. However, the king himself died in the sweltering heat of the Babylonian summer in 323 BC. So began the dizzying spiral of events that saw Antigonus and Demetrius rise to the height of Hellenistic power within just a decade.

Chapter 3

A Death in Babylon and the Rise of Demetrius

This chapter begins with Alexander's death in Babylon. It ends with Antigonus Monophthalmus and Demetrius in control of most of the great king's vast empire across two continents. Here I include some of the great events of Hellenistic history. These include the Partition of Babylon, the First War of the Diadochi, the Partition of Triparadeisos, and the Second War of the Diadochi. The latter concluded with two truly titanic battles at Paraitacene and Gabiene in modern Iran. Here the Antigonids finally defeated their chief rival, Eumenes of Cardia, making them undisputed masters of their world. Though only for the time being.

The Death of Alexander

When Alexander the Great died in Babylon on 10 June 323 BC he'd been suffering from a serious fever for ten days. The cause of death is uncertain, with the described symptoms indicating a ruptured ulcer or perhaps malaria, made worse through prodigious alcohol consumption early in the illness. Poison was also considered at the time, with some accusing Antipater's son Cassander (only recently arrived at court) of bringing it to Babylon, and his younger brother Iollas (the king's cup bearer) of administering it. Alexander's enemies in Athens certainly believed foul play was involved, later voting Iollas honours.

Whatever the cause, Alexander's last words had huge ramifications for decades afterwards. When asked to whom he would leave his kingdom, he said 'to the strongest'. Then, just before he died, Diodorus Siculus says his last words were 'I foresee that a great combat of my friends will be my funeral games'.[1] So it proved.

Alexander's unexpected death caused a huge outpouring of grief across his newly won empire. More importantly, he left no obvious heir. His first wife Roxanna was six months pregnant with the future Alexander IV, while another candidate was his elder half-brother, Philip Arrhidaeus. However, the latter had already been passed over for succession when Alexander became king due to a mental impairment of some kind. A more distant prospect was Alexander's supposed illegitimate son, Hercules. His mother was a Persian noblewoman named Barsine. She was the daughter of Artabazus, the Persian satrap of Phrygia whom Antigonus had replaced. Sadly, without a champion, none were a viable successor to the great king.

When Alexander died, many of the key players from the years of conquest were already gathered in Babylon, including his seven bodyguards who were also leading *strategoi* (commanders). These were Aristinous, Lysimachus, Peithon, Leonnatus, Ptolemy, Peucestas and Perdiccas. Other nobles present were Attalos, Demephon, Cleomenes, Menidas and Seleucus, who had all joined Peithon and Peucestas praying for the king's recovery the night before he died in a nearby temple of Serapis. Notable absent figures were Antipater, still regent in Macedon; Crateros, who was leading the veterans home and due to replace Antipater; and the 59-year-old Antigonus Monophthalmus with the 14-year-old Demetrius in Phrygia.

The Partition of Babylon

It was those now gathered around Alexander's body in Babylon who would determine who would wear Alexander's seal ring, the symbol of Macedonian kingship. Perdiccas rapidly emerged as the main player among those gathered. He was the *chiliarch* in charge of the first regiment of 1,000 Companion cavalrymen, and already Alexander's *de facto* second in command. Mindful that the army would insist on the Argead line continuing to rule, he wisely suggested he be regent until Roxanna's child was born. However, he then hesitated before putting the seal ring on his finger. This was a crucial error, given that the gathering was now being gate-crashed by the common foot soldiery, all keen to pay their respects to Alexander and have their say on the succession. Soon other options were being suggested, including appointing Arrhidaeus or Hercules king immediately. Chaos ensued, with blows exchanged over Alexander's corpse. Eventually, the king's bodyguards and nobles fled, having to leave the city for their safety. The cavalry followed.

A stand-off now took place, with the infantry inside Babylon and the nobles and cavalry outside. This turned into a siege. Eventually a compromise was reached, with Arrhidaeus becoming king as Phillip III, but sharing the throne with Roxanna's child if it was a boy. Perdiccas was then confirmed as regent, sharing this with Antipater in Macedon, who would then share his own regency with Craterus when he arrived in Pella with the veterans.

To celebrate the agreement, a traditional purification ceremony was arranged. However, the event was hijacked by Perdiccas who had no intention of honouring the agreement. He arranged for the foot troops and cavalry to stand on separate sides of the field chosen for the ceremony. That was normal procedure. When all was ready, amid great pomp he arrived with the new Macedonian elephant corps. Then, as soon as the ceremony began, he ordered the execution of the phalangite leaders who had supported Arrhidaeus or Hercules. The offenders were all seized and then trampled to death by the elephants in front of the whole gathered Macedonian soldiery.

Perdiccas then convened a new council, where he set out a new agreement more favourable to himself. Under this, the two kings (if the baby were a boy) would remain. However, he would be sole regent in Babylon, with Antipater and Crateros giving up any control over the kings. This gave Perdiccas the same powers as Alexander. Soon he was wearing the great king's seal ring. His first act was aimed at providing short term political stability, and to shore up his own reputation given his earlier hesitation. Here, he officially distributed control of the key regions and satrapies of Alexander's empire to the leading players among the nobility and army. The locations are important given they indicate the later individual power bases once the Wars of the Diadochi began.

- Antipater staying regent in Macedon, but reporting to Perdiccas, who would marry Antipater's daughter, Nicaea.
- Lysimachus given Thrace.
- Eumenes given Cappadocia.
- Leonnatus given Hellespontine-Phrygia.
- Antigonus Monophthalmus reconfirmed in Phrygia, and also given control of Pamphylia and Lycia. Demetrius to stay with him.
- Asander given Caria.
- Menander given Lydia.
- Philoxenus given Cilicia.
- Laomedon of Mytilene given Syria.
- Ptolemy at his own request given control of Egypt (see below).
- Neoptolemus given Armenia.
- Peucestas reconfirmed in Babylonia (where he commanded 20,000 Persian troops recruited under Alexander).
- Arcesilas reconfirmed in Mesopotamia.
- Antigines reconfirmed in Susiana.
- Pithon given Media, including all the territory up to the Caspian Gates.
- Tiepolemus (one of Alexander's *hetairoi*) reconfirmed in Carmania.
- Nicanor given Parthia.

- Stasanor given Aria and Drangiana.
- Archon given Pelasgia.
- Phillip reconfirmed in Hyrcania.
- Sibyrtius reconfirmed in Arachosia and Gedrosia.
- Amyntas reconfirmed in Bactria.
- Scythaeus reconfirmed in Sogdiana.
- Peithon, son of Agenor, reconfirmed in the satrapy of the Indus.

Meanwhile Crateros was given control of the royal treasury, and Seleucus command of the companion cavalry. This settlement was dubbed the Partition of Babylon, with Alexander's body now finally given its funeral rites and then preserved for transport back to Macedon.

What motivated these new powerbrokers as the Hellenistic world began? Certainly not philanthropy, or even loyalty to the Argeads. It was self-interest, pure and simple. As Green says;

> What these marshals wanted was colonial power, and the enormous fringe benefits that such power gave. Under their charismatic leader they had done what generations of pan Hellenists had advocated: they had conquered the Achaemenid empire of Persia. It had been a long, fierce, eleven-year struggle, and for all that time they had played subordinate roles to a new Achilles in pursuit of his heroic destiny. Now they wanted something more.[2]

Perdiccas was the clear winner in this first stage of the post-Alexandrian world. The son of a nobleman called Orontes from the leading Macedonian house of Orestis (the mountainous district between modern Greece and Macedonia), he was of similar age to Alexander. As a young man he was given command of his native battalion in the phalanx and accompanied Alexander in his campaigns in Illyria in 335 BC, and then a year later in Greece when he was severely injured during the siege of Thebes. He quickly recovered and accompanied the king throughout his campaigns in the East, becoming one of the seven bodyguards in 330 BC. His seniority is shown by the fact that when Alexander ordered his leading generals to marry Persian wives at Susa in 324 BC only four Macedonians married actual princesses, these being the king himself, his favourite Hephaestion, Crateros and Perdiccas. Well thought of as a military leader, Perdiccas then replaced Hephaestion as *chiliarch* of the first regiment of the companions when the latter died. This role also included being the king's vizier, his highest-ranking political adviser. And now, he was running Alexander's whole empire.

First War of the Diadochi and the Rise of the Antigonids

At first, the turmoil in the immediate aftermath of Alexander's death seemed to settle. At this point the Macedonian army was divided into three distinct components.

- Alexander's field army in Babylon, together with the garrison troops left across his newly conquered empire. These were under the control of Perdiccas.
- The home army in Macedon, able to call upon the Macedonian levy if needed. This was under the control of Antipater.
- The smaller armies of the various governors in Anatolia which contained troops left by Alexander to maintain lines of communication between the East and Macedon. This included that of Antigonus Monophthalmus.

All were soon to be set against each other. In Macedon, Antipater readily accepted the new status quo and offered Perdiccas the hand of his daughter Nicaea in marriage. However, he was then distracted by the Lamian War when opportunistic Athens led a rebellion against the League of Corinth. Leonnatus in Hellespontine-Phrygia and

Crateros, still with his veterans, came to his aid and soon the war was won.

Meanwhile Eumenes was having trouble securing Cappadocia, where a local king called Ariarathes was resisting orders to step down. Perdiccas commanded Antigonus to assist him, but the Phrygian governor refused. Plutarch says this was the first real sign of his independent ambition, a trait that would later see him and his son get to within touching distance of Alexander's crown. Aside from Perdiccas himself, this is also the first real example we have of political agency being shown by one of the Diadochi. As Plutarch explains, Antigonus 'was already lifted up in his own ambition and scorning all his associates'.[3] This is not surprising considering that Antigonus and Demetrius had spent a decade in the splendid isolation of their capital Celaenae, ruling the Phrygian population like kings while Alexander led his field army ever eastwards. Aside from regular dispatches and casualties from the front going west, and supplies and reinforcements from Macedon and Greece going east, the Antigonids had been left to their own devices. By the time Alexander died, they had clearly developed a taste for freedom of action. Further, they had no loyalty at all to the new political order set out in Babylon. If Antigonus looked to anyone, it would be Antipater in Macedon.

This was a challenge Perdiccas could not ignore. In late 322 BC he led the field army himself to Cappadocia, where he defeated and then executed Ariarathes, before officially installing Eumenes as the new governor there. He then headed further west, making camp on the border with Phrygia. There he summoned Antigonus to court, with a demand that he account for his actions. When Antigonus refused, his second rejection of a direct command, Perdiccas began a legal case against him. Soon Antigonus was charged with multiple counts of misadministration. However, the Phrygian governor was a wise and pragmatic man. He knew if he challenged Perdiccas in battle he'd be outnumbered. He therefore chose to play the long game, fleeing his beloved Celaenae in late 321 BC. Taking his family, including Demetrius, he headed for Europe. Arriving at Pella, he then delivered bombshell intelligence to Antipater. Perdiccas, having married the Macedonian regent's daughter Nicea, now planned to marry Alexander's sister Cleopatra. Diodorus Siculus is blunt about his scheming for the throne, saying:

> Perdiccas had formerly planned to work in harmony with Antipater, but when he gained control of the royal armies and the regency of the kings [Alexander IV had been born by this time], he changed his calculations. For since he was now reaching out for the kingship, he was bent on marrying Cleopatra, believing that he could use her to persuade the Macedonians to help him gain the supreme power.[4]

However, Perdiccas now overplayed his hand. Another royal marriage had been arranged in the aftermath of the agreement in Babylon. Here, Philip II's granddaughter, Eurydice, was to marry Arrhidaeus to help ensure the future security of the Argead line. Perdiccas viewed this as a likely challenge to his own growing ambitions. He therefore tried to intercept the girl as she travelled from Macedon to meet Arrhidaeus in Babylon. His mission was botched though, with Eurydice's mother, Cynane, being killed. At this news the field army revolted, forcing Perdiccas to back down. Arrhidaeus' marriage then proceeded as planned.

When this news reached Pella, Antigonus easily convinced Antipater that Perdiccas' next move would be to march on Macedon. Here, he was supported by Crateros, still in Pella after the Lamian War. Antipater, convinced, now wrote to Ptolemy in Alexandria to ask for his support. Thus was born a coalition featuring Antipater, Antigonus, Crateros and Ptolemy, all aligned to block the regal ambitions of Perdiccas. This marked the outbreak of the First War of the Diadochi.

Antigonus made the first move, returning to Anatolia with Demetrius at his side. They landed at Halicarnassus with 3,000 Macedonian troops provided from Antipater's home army. There Asander and Menander, the governors of Caria and of Lydia, joined him. Antigonus then secured the Ionian coastal cities, where he learned that Eumenes (by this time also appointed governor of Phrygia by Perdiccas) had seized the Lydian capital Sardis. From there he was acting as a message bearer between Cleopatra, still based there, and Perdiccas. Antigonus tried to ambush Eumenes with 2,000 of his best troops as they left Sardis but failed. Eumenes then fled back to Perdiccas. Antigonus next captured Sardis itself, where he reinstalled Menander as the governor. By the end of this short campaign, he'd secured the whole western seaboard of Anatolia, opening the way for his return to Phrygia.

The anti-Perdiccan alliance then opened a second Anatolian front, with Antipater and Crateros landing with their forces in Pamphylia on the southern Mediterranean coast. Here Perdiccas' growing unpopularity was evident, with the field army troops sent to oppose the landing (including the Armenian governor Neoptolemus, another of Alexander's old generals) deserting en masse.

Then more shocking news reached Perdiccas, this time from Syria. There, Ptolemy had mounted a stunning *coup de main*, seizing Alexander's body in its grand catafalque as it travelled back to Macedon. He carefully diverted the cortege to Egypt where the king's body was laid to rest at Memphis in a pharaoh's burial. Why did Ptolemy mount such a spectacular heist? He later claimed it was to protect Alexander's legacy, and with its ultimate resting place being the grand *Soma* mausoleum in Alexandria (built by his son Ptolemy II Philadelphus), this he certainly achieved. Here, it was set on permanent display in a gold coffin from around 274 BC, the ultimate quasi-magical good-luck charm and legitimizer of power.

However, there is a clear wider pattern to all of Ptolemy's actions, a man fiercely loyal to Alexander in his lifetime but who was also a wise and canny political operator. He had already foreseen the likely disintegration of the king's empire as the generals squabbled around his body in Babylon, hence his choice of Egypt in the Babylonian partition. There, in a very defensible and wealthy part of the Hellenistic world, he could build his own empire. Which he did, with Alexander's body his greatest trophy.

For now, though, he was still aligned with his allies across the Mediterranean against Perdiccas. The latter, justifiably paranoid, tried to get the field army to condemn Ptolemy, arguing that the latter was trying to set himself up as king of the whole empire (in fact, the last thing Ptolemy wanted). When this failed, he then turned to Ptolemy's deputy, Cleomenes, encouraging him to betray the Egyptian governor. This was easier than it sounds given that Cleomenes had been demoted from being governor himself to make way for Ptolemy. However, Ptolemy quickly got wind of this and the unlucky Cleomenes was soon eliminated, the first of the Diadochi to die.

Perdiccas now determined to deal with Ptolemy once and for all. In spring 320 BC he marched south to Egypt, leaving the defence and government of Asia to Eumenes. Greek by birth and a native of Cardia in the Thracian Chersonese, the latter had served Philip II as private secretary, a role he continued under Alexander until promoted commander of a *hipparchia* of companion cavalry. Now, as a successor *strategos*, he became the Antigonids' foremost opponent.

To the south, Perdiccas' campaign was a fiasco, with 2,000 men drowning while trying to cross the Nile. That was the final straw for the regent's demoralized army, his own officers assassinating him on 20 May. The first blow was struck by Antigenes, commander of the Argyraspides (Silver Shields) guard regiment, formerly Alexander's Hypaspsists.

Ptolemy, waiting on the west bank of the river, now crossed and entered the field army camp to great acclaim, not least because he distributed food among the Perdiccan soldiers who were on short rations. He shrewdly avoided taking any responsibility for the two kings, with Peithon and a fellow *strategos* called Arrhidaeus appointed as short-term regents.

Meanwhile, in Anatolia, Antipater, Antigonus and Crateros had taken advantage of the field army's absence to attack Eumenes. To everyone's surprise they were rebuffed, with Crateros killed. This was a double-edged sword for the Perdiccans given that Crateros had been very popular with the Macedonians. Indeed, when the field army on the banks of the Nile heard the news they reacted with fury, killing Perdiccas' sister Atalante (wife of his general Attalus) and many of his supporters in the camp. They then condemned Eumenes and fifty of his chief supporters to death. With matters now getting out of hand, Ptolemy escorted the field army back to Syria, except for some troops who chose to remain in Egypt.

The 'field army' arrived at Triparadeisos in upper Syria in late summer 320 BC in volatile mood, having marched north without pay. There Peithon and the general Arrhidaeus summoned Antipater, Antigonus and Seleucus (who appears as a prominent successor here for the first time) to join Ptolemy to work on a new settlement. However, high drama again intervened.

This was in the form of King Arrhidaeus' ambitious wife Eurydice, who amid the drama of Perdiccas' downfall saw an opportunity to advance her husband's cause. She stirred up the army to demand an immediate cash payment, at which point Peithon and the general Arrhidaeus resigned, with the 80-year-old Antipater appointed guardian of the kings, though he had yet to arrive from Macedon. Once at Triparadeisos, and accompanied by Antigonus, he wisely set up a camp for his own 'home army' troops away from the mutinous 'field army', forewarned of events. He then entered the latter's camp, only to be met by demands for immediate payment again, with Eurydice whipping the troops up once more. The ageing regent tried to calm them with a promise to search the nearby Persian royal treasuries for their pay, but this was rejected. A riot ensued in which Antipater was almost stoned to death. It was Antigonus who saved the day, with Polyaenus providing vivid detail:

> Antigonus, who advised him to leave the camp, undertook to assist his escape. Antigonus accordingly crossed the bridge in full armour, and rode directly through the phalanx, thereby dividing it; he turned first to one division, and then to the other, as if he was going to harangue them. The Macedonians paid every attention due his rank and character; and followed him with great interest, to hear what he had to offer. As soon as they formed around him, he began a long harangue in defence of Antipater; promising, assuring, and urging every consideration to induce them to wait patiently, until he should be in a situation in which he could satisfy their demands. During this prolix harangue, Antipater crossed the bridge with some horsemen; and thus escaped the soldiers' resentment.[5]

Seleucus was also involved here, with his cavalry sent to put down the rebellious field army. They quickly succeeded, with the rebellion crushed and Eurydice silenced. Antipater then called a new assembly. Here he was officially appointed supreme regent of the whole empire, with specific control of Greece, and confirmed as guardian of both Arrhidaeus and Alexander IV. He then carried out a new partition of the satrapies, with the key appointments detailed below (again broadly west to east):

- Lysimachus reconfirmed in Thrace.
- Nicanor given Eumenes' old satrapy of Cappadocia.
- The general Arrhidaeus given Hellespontine-Phrygia.

- Antigonus Monophthalmus reconfirmed in Phrygia, Pamphylia and Lycia, and appointed the new commander of the field army in Asia, an enormous advancement making him the second most powerful figure of the era after Antipater. Again, Demetrius stayed with him, this time as his formal second in command.
- Asander reconfirmed in Caria.
- Cleitus given Lydia.
- Philoxenus reconfirmed in Cilicia.
- Laomedon of Mytilene reconfirmed in Syria.
- Ptolemy remaining in Egypt, where Diodorus Siculus describes him as already immovable.[6]
- Seleucus given Babylonia, a huge step up for him.
- Amphimachus given Mesopotamia and Arbelitis.
- Antigenes given Susiana.
- Peucestas being given Persia, having been moved from Babylonia to accommodate Seleucus.
- Pithon reconfirmed in Media.
- Tiepolemus reconfirmed in Carmania.
- Phillip being given Parthia.
- Stasander the Cypriot being given Aria and Drangiana.
- Sibyrtius reconfirmed in Arachosia and Gedrosia.
- Stasanor being moved to Bactria and Sogdiana, a post none of the Macedonians would accept this time.
- Peithon, son of Agenor, reconfirmed in the satrapy of the Indus.

We see in this settlement Indian kings also appearing for the first time, with Alexander's old opponent Porus being confirmed king of the non-Macedonian Indian territories in the Punjab, and 'Taxiles the Indian' being confirmed as king of the territories between the Indus and Hydaspes. Peace now descended across the Hellenistic world as the key players returned to their territories to consolidate their positions. It would not last for long.

It was around this time that Antigonus celebrated his ascension to the very top of Hellenistic power by founding a new city which was later to be the location of an event still profound today. This was Antigoneia in Bithynia near the Sea of Marmara, today modern İznik. Later, after Antigonus' final defeat, it was captured by Lysimachus who renamed it Nicaea to celebrate his victory. It remained so into the Roman period. It was here that Constantine I convened the First Council of Nicaea in AD 325, where the Nicene Creed was agreed as the basis of worship in the Catholic Church, as it remains today.

Second War of the Diadochi, Enter Demetrius

The two leading Diadochi were now Antipater and Antigonus. They sealed their political alliance through the marriage of Antipater's daughter Phila (Crateros' widow) to Demetrius. This is the first time our protagonist emerges onto the historical stage in his own right, and not in a flattering way. It seems likely that he was with his father at every key stage of the events which led to the Partition of Triparadeisos and was still enjoying the high life as a good-looking man with immense prospects. Plutarch adds fine vignettes from this time, saying:

> On one occasion, when Demetrius had been at his revels for several days, and excused his absence by saying that he was troubled with a flux, 'So I learned', said Antigonus, 'but was it Thasian or Chian wine that flowed?' And again, learning that his son was sick, Antigonus was going to see him, and met a certain beauty at his door; he went in, however, sat down by his son, and felt his pulse. 'The fever has left me now', said Demetrius. 'No doubt, my boy,' said Antigonus, 'I met it just now at the door as it was going away.'[7]

However, Plutarch adds that, when not carousing, Demetrius proved an excellent deputy for his father. He was clearly able to keep the two extremes of his life separate, as Plutarch explains:

> These failings of Demetrius were treated with such lenity by his father because the young man was so efficient otherwise. The Scythians, in the midst of their drinking and carousing, twang their bow-strings, as though summoning back their courage when it is dissolved in pleasure; but Demetrius, giving himself up completely, now to pleasure, and now to duty, and keeping the one completely separate from the other, was no less formidable in his preparations for war.[8]

One thing is clear now though. The 19-year-old Demetrius did not want to marry the Macedonian matron who was suddenly thrust upon him as a bride. As one modern commenator puts it:

> A sober, serious woman more than twice his age, twice widowed and with children from both unions, was certainly not the bride Demetrius would have sought, had he even wanted to wed.[9]

However, from Antigonus' point of view, she was a fabulous catch for the wider family given that it bonded him firmly to Antipater. For now, Demetrius would have to man up and do his bit for the family firm. We have no details about the wedding, which likely took place in 319 BC, but soon Phila was pregnant and gave birth to a son named Antigonus after his grandfather. He would prove to be the most important of the Antigonids given it was he who established a sustainable dynasty on the Macedonian throne. Today we call him Antigonus 'Gonatus' (the Knock-kneed). It would be intriguing to know the origins of this enigmatic epithet. Sadly we do not.

Antigonus Monophthalmus was soon in action, with Antipater tasking him with hunting down the now sentenced-to-death Eumenes and any surviving Perdiccan supporters. So began the Second War of the Diadochi. For this Antigonus not only had the 'field army' with 70 elephants, but also a substantial part of the 'home army', including 8,500 foot and 8,500 allied cavalry. He was also joined by Antipater's son Cassander, who was no doubt tasked with keeping an eye on things for the regent.

By this time the Perdiccans had established a power base in western Anatolia, threatening to cut off Alexander's Asian territory from Macedon. Eumenes had occupied Hellespontine Phrygia, Perdiccas' brother Alcetas had gathered an army in Pisidia, while Attalus (husband of the murdered Atalante) attacked Rhodes with the royal fleet, which had stayed loyal to the Perdiccans. While the latter was defeated at sea by the Rhodians, Alcetas was far more successful, defeating the Carian governor Asander, who Antipater had sent to challenge him.

Next, Eumenes headed south along the coast, extorting the Ionian Greek cities there and raiding the royal horse stud at Mount Ida. He then marched on Sardis, scene of his failed brokering of a marriage between Perdiccas and Cleopatra, his intention being to win her over for himself. However, his path was blocked by Antipatrid troops and he reverted to a guerrilla campaign which proved highly successful. By that point Antipater had arrived back in Pella with both kings and their respective royal families. They were never to set foot in Asia again.

At this point, with their fortunes on the up, the Perdiccans crucially failed to unite. This would prove their undoing as Antigonus and Demetrius now arrived. Their first target was Eumenes, by this time wintering in Cappadocia. There he was already suffering from an issue which would plague him as he fought the Antigonids: desertion, stemming from the fact that he was Greek and not Macedonian. When faced with 3,000 of his phalangites declaring their intention to return to Macedon, he had to execute the ring leaders before they rejoined his ranks.

Antigonus forced an initial engagement near the Cappadocian town of Orcyni. Here he was outnumbered, with 10,000 foot (including a veteran Macedonian pike phalanx of 5,000 men), 2,000 cavalry and 30 war elephants. Against this Eumenes fielded 20,000 infantry

The Parthenon atop the Acropolis in Athens. Scene of much debauchery during Demetrius' second stay in the city.

The Erechtheion ionic temple atop the Acropolis. Its famous Porch of the Caryatids has greeted visitors to the Parthenon for centuries.

The author on the harbourside at Piraeus, the port of Athens, at the scene where Demetrius leapt ashore on his first stay to the city.

The agora, Athens. The Parthenon can be seen atop the Acropolis at top right.

The Alexander Mosaic from the House of the Faun in Pompeii, now in the National Archaeological Museum, Naples, undergoing restoration. The Argead hammer and anvil in action, Alexander and Companions to the left, pikemen to the right, as Darius III flees.

Recreation of the Alexander Mosaic. (*National Archaeological Museum, Naples*)

Lysimachus, nemesis of Antigonus and Demetrius at the Battle of Ipsus. (*National Archaeological Museum, Naples*)

Seleucus I Nicator, the Successor who held Demetrius in luxurious captivity at the end of his life. (*National Archaeological Museum, Naples*)

Theatre, Ephesus. Where Demetrius fled to with his surviving troops after the disastrous Antigonid defeat at Ipsus.

Temple of Apollo, Didyma (modern Didim), one of the key religious sites on the Ionian Greek coast of western Anatolia, frequently visited by Successors.

Wargaming the Wars of the Diadochi. Silver Shields and pikemen with armoured elephants and skirmishers. (*Author's collection*)

Silver Shield Macedonian guard phalangite. (*Author's collection*)

The price of failure in the Hellenistic world. Badly damaged pikeman's Pilos helmet, Vatican Museum.

Classical and Hellenistic Greek elite armour on display in a tomb from Paestum, Campania. Thracian helmet, greaves and muscled cuirass. A very expensive panoply.

Defensive panoply of a less well armed Greek warrior. Here at right a hoplite fights a local Lucanian, Paestum, Campania.

Trireme galley wall painting, originally from Pompeii, now in the National Archaeological Museum, Naples. War galleys with multiple banks of oars were the ubiquitous warship of the Classical Greek and Hellenistic worlds.

Europe and Asia depicted on a wall painting from Pompeii, now in the National Archaeological Museum, Naples. Note Europe is represented by a Hellenistic phalangite.

Bust of Alexander the Great or Demetrius, British Museum.

Demetrius the Besieger, National Archaeological Museum, Naples.

Bust of Hellenistic elite cavalryman, National Archaeological Museum, Naples.

and 5,000 cavalry. However, Antigonus bribed one of Eumenes's cavalry commanders, Appollonides, to desert once the engagement began. Polyaenus says he then deployed two brilliant stratagems. First, he had a messenger arrive covered in dust during an embassy with Eumenes' herald to announce that 'allied reinforcements' were close by, to which Antigonus reacted with mock delight. Next, in the prelude to battle the following morning, Antigonus lengthened his line by deploying his phalanx eight men deep instead of the usual 16 to give the impression the allies had already arrived. Eumenes fell for the trick, acting cautiously when the advantage really lay with him, and only engaging with his light troops.[10] Then, at a crucial moment when Eumenes decided to commit to the battle, Appollonides defected as planned and attacked his own side, winning the day for the Antigonids. The result was a decisive victory for Antigonus and Demetrius, they capturing Eumene's supply train and killing 8,000 men, with the Greek leader and his surviving men then fleeing east for Armenia.

Antigonus, sensing a campaign victory, mounted a vigorous pursuit, though was hampered by Eumenes again resorting to guerilla warfare. However, his opponent was once more beset by large scale desertions. Therefore, he decided to make a stand with his 600 most loyal troops at the mountain fortress of Nora in southern Cappadocia. There the two protagonists met face-to-face outside its walls, Antigonus having to protect his former friend from his own Macedonians angered by the death of Crateros at the Hellespont. Offer and counter offer were made, Antigonus keen not to get dragged into a lengthy siege and knowing he already had control of most of Eumenes' territory. In the end Antigonus offered to lift the siege if Eumenes acknowledged him as his superior, while the latter demanded Cappadocia be given back to him and his death sentence lifted. Antigonus referred this potential settlement back to Antipater in Pella, keen to move on. In the meantime, he agreed a truce with Eumenes while he awaited instructions.

Antigonus was an old man in a hurry, and acted accordingly. Leaving a besieging force to keep Eumenes contained, he marched 450km in seven days with his remaining troops to force a meeting engagement with Alcetas in what became known as the Battle of Pisidia. Here he vastly outnumbered his Perdiccan opponent, with 40,000 foot (including many Macedonian deserters from Eumenes, doubling the size of his phalanx), 7,000 horse and 70 elephants. This huge force surprised Alcetas by occupying the high ground above his camp, forcing the Perdiccan to rashly charge his 900 cavalry uphill to try to buy time to deploy his 16,000 foot (including 6,000 Pisidian light troops). These were beaten in quick time, Antigonus then charging his phalanx and elephants downhill to smash through Alcetas' centre, while his cavalry under Demetrius marauded around his opponent's flanks. Total victory soon followed, with many of Alcetas' Macedonians deserting to Antigonus. The Perdiccan fled to nearby Termessos with his bodyguard and his Pisidians. Here the local town elders murdered him, despite the younger Pisidians wanting to stay loyal. Antigonus then took his body and, to make a statement, brutalized it. Diodorus Siculus provides the details, saying:

> He maltreated it for three days: then as the corpse began to decay, he threw it out unburied and departed from Pisidia.[11]

The body was eventually buried by the young men of the town, with the tomb of Alcetas still visible today in the ruins of Termessus. Meanwhile, the victorious Antigonus and Demetrius returned to Phrygia and their palace at Celaenae to see out the winter. Their growing prowess was not lost on their competitors, with Antigonus now showing overt ambition. Diodorus Siculus says:

> He aspired to greater things: for there were no longer any commanders in all Asia who had an army strong enough to compete with him for

> supremacy. Therefore, although maintaining for the time a pretence of being well disposed toward Antipater, he had decided that, as soon as he had made his own position secure, he would no longer take orders from either the 'kings' or from Antipater.[12]

Here events overtook him. In late 319 BC Antipater died of old age at 81. This dragged Macedon and Greece into the Second War of the Diadochi proper, given Antipater's son Cassander refused to accept his father's decision to nominate the old *strategos* Polyperchon as his successor.

The regent's death left Antigonus pre-eminent among the successors, particularly in his Asian powerbase. There, he was now able to field an immense 70,000 strong force, including a sizeable elephant corps. Further, at Sardis he had access to the largest treasury of any of the successors. Thus, if more troops were needed, hiring mercenaries would be no problem. However, his opponents knew all this too. Soon, they began to actively move against him.

First to make a move was the general Arrhidaeus in Hellespontine-Phrygia, the crucial steppingstone from Asia to Europe. Fearful Antigonus would remove his satrapy, he decided to garrison the Ionian Greek cities in his realm. Knowing they would protest, he marched on Cyzicus, determined to make an example of it by means of an army of 12,000 mercenaries and a large siege train. On arrival he demanded the city's surrender. It refused and a siege began. Antigonus reacted with lightning speed, selecting his best 23,000 troops and force-marching them to the city. There he found the locals had already beaten off Arrhidaeus, who'd withdrawn to his nearby camp. Antigonus accused him of rebellion and demanded he surrender. Arrhidaeus refused and sent a force to free Eumenes, still within the fortress at Nora.

As before, Antigonus decided to pick off his opponents one by one. In the first instance he targeted Cleitus, Eumenes' ally in Lydia who, realizing his position was hopeless, fled to Pella after garrisoning his cities. Antigonus, ascendant, was unstoppable, quickly capturing Ephesus where he seized a convoy in the harbour carrying 600 talents of silver. The other Lydian cities fell soon after, with Antigonus at this point approaching Cassander with an offer to support him against Polyperchon if he agreed to an alliance. Cassander readily accepted. With another successful campaigning season over, Antigonus and Demetrius then withdrew back to Celaenae to winter with his army.

Early in 318 BC Antigonus decided to secure his position in Anatolia, reaching out to Eumenes still besieged in Nora, offering peace for loyalty. According to Diodorus Siculus, his former friend readily accepted, keen to escape Nora's dank walls and giving an oath-bound pledge to be Antigonus' ally, though Plutarch adds that Eumenes changed the wording to include loyalty to the joint kings and Olympias too.[13] Whatever the truth, Eumenes returned to Cappadocia with Antigonus' good will.

However, trouble was on the way for the Antigonids. Polyperchon, casting around for allies to help him secure the Macedonian regency, alighted on Eumenes. He wrote to him, saying that in the kings' names the Greek had been given control of the satrapy of Cilicia in addition to Cappadocia. Polyperchon also offered him troops and 500 talents of silver from the treasury in Cilicia. The former, crucially, included the 3,000 Argyraspides (Silver Shields). Eumenes was torn here, having made his peace with Antigonus and enjoying the novelty of newfound security. Ever a loyalist to the royal cause though, he finally sided with Polyperchon, launching his last attempt at power and fame.

Antigonus reacted with cold fury. As Eumenes bolted for Cilicia and Polyperchon's treasure, Antigonus tried to arrest him, but his troops arrived three days too late. Once in Cilicia, Eumenes was joined by the

Argyraspides' commander Antigenes, governor of Susiana, the scene now set for the campaign which was to lead to the two great set-piece battles of the Second War of the Diadochi.

Once more, Eumenes had difficulty with the loyalty of the Macedonians in his army, including Antigenes, who Plutarch says feigned his allegiance to the Greek. He therefore resorted to a stratagem of his own to keep control of his disparate army, claiming to have had a dream where Alexander had appeared to him, telling him no business was to be carried out in the name of the kings unless in a royal tent to be called the Pavilion of Alexander. He then produced a golden throne. From that moment he received all visitors and held counsel only in that tent and on that throne.[14] In effect, he was claiming to be acting on behalf on the ghost of Alexander, a ruse which in the short term worked.

Having shored up his support, Eumenes now started recruiting more troops using his newly gathered treasure, eventually amassing a force of 18,000 including the elite Argyraspides. However, at this point Ptolemy reappears, no doubt encouraged by Antigonus, with his fleet anchoring off the Cilician coast. There it landed a delegation which reached out to Eumenes' army to encourage its defection. The attempt failed, with the Greek's subterfuge regarding Alexander keeping the troops in line for now.

Next, Antigonus tried a subterfuge of his own, sending his friend Philotas to bribe Antigenes away from Eumenes with the Argyraspides. However, he stayed loyal. Philotas then tried to persuade the other Macedonians in the army to seize and kill Eumenes, this time with the threat of Antigonus arriving with his entire army if they did not. Eumenes himself intervened here though, convincing his troops to remain loyal.

Polyperchon now moved to support his ally Eumenes, sending the Macedonian fleet against Antigonus under Cleitus. Antigonus' deployed his own fleet, bolstered by ships sent by Cassander under the command of Nicanor. This gave him a force of 130 war galleys. The two fleets met off Byzantium, with Cleitus the victor, capturing 70 vessels. However, Antigonus responded to the reverse quickly. That night he deployed his light troops around the bay near Byzantium where the victorious Cleitus had beached his ships. Polyaenus describes the ensuing action, saying:

> At day break a shower of javelins and arrows was poured upon the enemy. While they were just arising, and scarcely awake, they were seriously injured, before they realized where the attack was coming from. Some cut their cables, and others weighed their anchors. Nothing prevailed but noise and confusion. Antigonus at the same time ordered the sixty ships [he had left] to bear down upon them. Under attack both from the sea, and from land, the conquerors were obliged to yield their victory to the conquered.[15]

Only Cleitus' own ship escaped the catastrophe, with Antigonus once more seizing the initiative. The Perdiccan was captured shortly afterwards by Lysimachus and executed, another Successor dead. Antigonus, now leaving the conflict in Europe to Cassander, marched on Eumenes with 20,000 foot, his fleet hugging the Anatolian coast to cover his littoral flank. Eumenes wisely fled with his most loyal troops, including the Argyraspides, to Phoenicia, with the idea of opening a new front in the war, this time against Ptolemy. However, failing to force a meeting engagement, he took the fateful decision to march eastwards again, this time into the heart of the empire, where he hoped to find new support.

There, Pithon in Media had been defeated by his neighbouring satraps while trying to expand his power base, fleeing to Babylon where he convinced Seleucus to side with him. Their chief opponent was Peucestas, satrap of Persia and no friend of Seleucus given the latter had forced him out his original satrapy at Triparadisus. Eumenes knew that if he could win over one of these factions it would give him access to a new source of troops. He decided to reach out to Pithon and Seleucus, as they had 23,000 men and over 120 war elephants. He marched to Babylon and went into winter quarters there, sending embassies to the Median and Babylonian governors. However, they rebuffed him and tried to convince Antigenes to turn against him. Once more, though, Antigenes remained faithful.

Meanwhile, to the west, Antigonus and Demetrius had set off in hot pursuit. Soon they were in Mesopotamia, where they set up their own winter quarters. In the spring of 317 BC they headed east again, arriving in Babylon to find Eumenes gone. Seleucus told them the Greek had done a deal with Peucestas and had gone even further east to meet up with the combined armies of the eastern satrapies. In total the Greek now fielded 34,000 foot and 8,000 cavalry. The former included the Argyraspides. Further, Eumenes had paid his Macedonian troops six months' salary in advance to secure their loyalty.

The Battles of Paraitacene and Gabiene

Antigonus waited until the summer to march after Eumenes, enlisting Pithon and Seleucus who provided additional troops, particularly infantry and elephants. Eumenes himself was bolstered by the arrival of the new Indian satrap Eudamos, a general in the service of Porus who had assassinated the Indian king the year before and taken control of much of his territory. He bought with him 125 well-trained Indian war elephants.

However, Eumenes was still outnumbered by the Antigonids and chose to head even further east, hoping for reinforcements from Bactria and Sogdiana. When these failed to materialize he knew he would have to fight and turned back to face the Antigonids. Their dogged pursuit finally paid dividends, with the great rivals meeting in battle at Paraitacene, northeast of Susa in modern Iran.

Eumene's army had a particularly eastern flavour. It included a 17,000-strong phalanx, with the Argyraspides forming its core; 18,000 light troops, including 10,000 Persian archers and slingers of dubious loyalty; 6,300 cavalry and Eudamos' elephants. Meanwhile, Antigonus fielded a larger phalanx of 28,000, with 11,000 cavalry but fewer elephants.

Eumenes occupied a position with his left flank resting on high ground where he deployed a force of cavalry, mostly light horse, commanded by Eudamos. In the centre he deployed the phalanx in a solid line with the Argyraspides to the left, and with his light troops ahead and on either side. On the right he deployed his shock cavalry, with him in charge (though he was ill during the battle and carried in a litter). His large elephant corps was deployed across the front of his entire line.

Meanwhile the wily Antigonus positioned himself on even higher ground, from where he was able to observe Eumene's entire deployment. He acted accordingly, deploying his force obliquely, with the right wing leading (including most of the lance-armed shock cavalry and elephants) under his own command. Demetrius, now 20 and fighting his first large set-piece battle, was at his side. On the left he deployed most of the light cavalry under Pithon, with the phalanx in steps across his centre.

The engagement began with Pithon's light horse skirmishing forward to engage Eumenes' force across its entire front, with orders to avoid frontal contact. The aim here was to screen Antigonus' right-flank oblique attack which was forming behind. However, Eumenes reacted quickly, with his own light horse dispersing Pithon's troops with a flanking attack, though this made his left dangerously weak. This flank then fell back ahead of Antigonus' shock cavalry, avoiding contact.

Next the phalanxes engaged where, despite their fewer numbers, Eumenes' troops got the upper hand, particularly the Argyraspides. Soon Antigonus' phalangites were being pushed back. Then, just at the point the battle was turning against Antigonus, a large gap opened in Eumenes' phalanx as the Silver Shields pursued their retiring opponents too vigorously. Antigonus immediately charged his shock cavalry and elephants through the gap, hitting Eumenes's phalanx on its exposed inner flanks. Units of his cavalry then wheeled left through the gap and behind the phalanx to hit Eumenes' own right flank cavalry in the rear. At this point Eumenes recalled his own light horse which were pursuing Pithon. This gave Antigonus enough time to rally his own light horse, and the units of his phalanx that had been falling back. With nighttime coming, Eumenes decided it was better to fight another day rather than perish, and withdrew his remaining troops, including the Argyraspides, back to his fortified camp. Antigonus claimed victory because he remained on the battlefield, though he'd lost more men. As the day closed, he then deployed one final stratagem to disguise his losses to Eumenes. Polyaenus says:

> Eumenes sent a herald to Antigonus to arrange with him a mutual agreement to bury their dead. Antigonus, who had been informed that his own loss exceeded that of the enemy, to conceal the fact, detained the herald, until his own dead had been cremated. After they had been buried, he let the herald go and agreed to the proposal.[16]

With the year end approaching, both armies now settled into their winter quarters, Eumenes at Gabiene in central Persia, Antigonus in Media.

However, if the troops thought the campaigning season over, they were wrong. As 317 BC drew to a close, word reached Antigonus that a mutiny had broken out in Eumene's army again. His agents told him that the Greek's troops had spread themselves out far and wide across the territory of Gabiene in disparate camps, some of them six days' march apart. Eumene's subsequent order for the troops to concentrate were ignored. This presented a unique opportunity to surprise Eumenes, and Antigonus eagerly grabbed it.

Gathering his army, Antigonus showed true strategic skill once more, deciding to approach Gabiene from an unexpected direction. This was across a desert plain littered with bogs and sulphur mines, avoiding an easier route patrolled by Eumenes' scouts. Before setting out, Antigonus gave orders that all his troops should only take food that required no cooking. He then leaked misinformation to Eumenes' camp that he intended to retire north to Armenia. Then, on the winter solstice in December 317 BC, he set out, issuing further orders that no fires were to be lit at night.

Antigonus' troops suffered much hardship during this march, given it took place in the freezing cold of a desert winter. By the fifth night some troops had had enough and disobeyed orders, lighting fires which were seen by Eumenes's agents. The latter now sought to buy time while he tried to gather his army. Here he used a clever stratagem of his own. This involved lighting thousands of campfires at the edge of the desert to give Antigonus the impression his opponent's full force had already gathered. Antigonus continued on regardless, discovering the ruse as he reached the desert's edge. He then plundered the surrounding countryside to feed his men.

Antigonus next tried to capture Eumene's sizeable elephant corps which had been slow to join the rest of his army. He narrowly failed. Both sides now decided an engagement was inevitable and prepared for battle. On the day itself Eumenes' spies discovered Antigonus' plan of deployment. The Greek acted accordingly, positioning his best mounted troops on his left, opposite Antigonus and Demetrius. This included his own guard cavalry, those of the eastern satraps, 60 of his elephants and some supporting light troops. His foot numbered 36,700, again with a large proportion of native light troops. These were deployed in his centre, while on his right Philip (the governor of Parthia) commanded the remainder of his 6,000 cavalry. The rest of his 114 elephants were deployed in line across his centre and left.

Meanwhile Antigonus had a phalanx of 22,000, some light troops, 9,000 cavalry and 65 elephants. Again he deployed his best lance-armed shock cavalry on his right, this time nominally under Demetrius, though he commanded the wing himself. His phalanx was deployed in the centre, while Pithon again commanded the light horse on the left flank. This time his elephant corps was spread out across his whole frontage. Thus the two armies had their strongest wings opposite each other.

Before the battle opened, Antigenes, the Argyraspides' commander, crossed the battlefield on his charger to heckle the Antigonid phalanx, according to Diodorous saying:

> Wicked men, are you sinning against your fathers, who conquered the whole world under Philip and Alexander?[17]

The morale of Antigonus' phalanx suffered at this, while Eumenes' phalangites raised a great cheer. The Greek *strategos* saw his opportunity and began a general advance, with the light troops of both sides opening the battle with a general exchange. Next, both elephant lines charged the other, fighting tusk to tusk, kicking up a large dust cloud which Antigonus now used to his advantage, ordering his left-flank light cavalry under Pithon to carry out a wide flanking movement to Eumenes' rear, dramatically capturing the latter's baggage train. Meanwhile, on the right and again using the dust cloud as cover, Antigonus and Demetrius rode around the engaged elephants to their front and struck Eumenes' own left-wing cavalry in the flank, causing mayhem. After a short, stiff fight, Eumenes' ally Peucestas was routed along with his 1,500 Persian cavalry, only halting when they reached a secure position to the rear.

However, the battle of the phalanxes was a different matter. Led by the Argyraspides, Eumenes' phalanx smashed into the Antigonid centre and drove straight through it. Diodorus Siculus colourfully reports that the Silver Shields:

> were not to be checked in their charge and engaged the entire opposing phalanx, showing themselves so superior in skill and strength that of their own men they lost not one, but of those who opposed them they slew over 5,000 and routed the entire force of foot soldiers, whose numbers were many times their own.[18]

Eumenes now saw his chance. Though bested on both left and right, he'd secured the centre and quickly ordered Peucestas back into line to exploit the gap there with his cavalry. However, to Eumenes' horror, the Persian governor refused to move. Antigonus, seeing this, then ordered Pithon's horse, just returned from plundering Eumenes' camp, to attack the Argyraspides in the rear. The veterans calmly ceased their pursuit of the Antigonid centre and formed a huge square with their attached light troops in the centre, safely marching from the field of battle. This effectively marked the end of the engagement, Antigonus again claiming possession of the battlefield, but with both sides effectively fighting each other to a standstill.

That evening, Eumenes attempted to convince his commanders that Antigonus should be engaged anew the following morning, but they were reluctant given their families were among the captured baggage train. Both armies now stood off each other for three days. The Macedonians in Eumenes' army then reached out to Antigonus to demand the return of their families and baggage. Antigonus responded with a proclamation, saying he'd let every soldier recover his property without ransom. This had a dramatic effect on Eumenes' army, with Polyaenus saying:

> Many of Eumenes' men immediately revolted to Antigonus' side, these not only Macedonians, but also 10,000 Persians under the command of Peucestas. For as soon as he saw that the Macedonians inclined to Antigonus, he followed their example.[19]

Pandemonium now broke out in Eumenes' camp, with his troops streaming away to join Antigonus. The Greek leader tried one final time to rally his soldiers to his cause. His fate was finally sealed by the Argyraspides who saw how things would end. Plutarch has one of them say:

> Pay no attention to his babbling; for it was not so dreadful a thing … that a pest from the Chersonesus should come to grief for having harassed Macedonians with infinite wars, as that the best of the soldiers of Philip and Alexander, after all their toils, should in their old age be robbed of their rewards and get their support from others, and that their wives should be spending the third night now in the arms of their enemies.[20]

With that they grabbed Eumenes, wrapped him in chains and dragged him to the Antigonid camp. There, after a few days deliberating what to do with his captive, Antigonus removed Eumenes' chains and allowed his friends to visit him one last time. He then had him executed, along with Eudamos and Antigenes. Meanwhile the rest of the Argyraspides, far from being rewarded for their treachery, were sent by Antigonus to the far-off satrapy of Arachosia in modern Afghanistan. There the governor Sibyrtius was given specific orders to send them out on dangerous missions to ensure they didn't return. Such was the end for Alexander's elite foot guard corps.

This brought an end to the Second War of the Diadochi, a conflict that spanned the entirety of Alexander's empire, with Antigonus now the undisputed master. It was also the conflict which saw Demetrius emerge from his father's shadow, a process now accelerated as the Antigonids began paying the price for their astonishing success.

Chapter 4
Antigonids Ascendent

Peace among the Successors didn't last long, and soon the Hellenistic warlords were again at war. However, as their conflicts progressed through the Third and Fourth Wars of the Diadochi, a brutal edge began to emerge, with each leader fighting for their very survival. Both conflicts are covered in depth here, with Demetrius now leading his own fleets and armies on campaign and in battle.

Rise of the Antipatrids

By this time two dramatic events had occurred in the Balkans that changed the Hellenistic world forever. These were Olympias' murder of the first of the 'kings', Alexander's elder brother Arrhidaeus (now styled Philip III), and then the subsequent murder of Olympias herself by Cassander.

In the first instance, Polyperchon succeeded Antipater as regent when the latter died in 319 BC. However, Antipater's son Cassander quickly manoeuvred to replace Polyperchon and by 318 BC had established Arrhidaeus as the sole Macedonian king. As detailed in Chapter 3, here he was helped with his alliance with Antigonus in Asia, who was still in the endgame of his war with Eumenes. Polyperchon was forced out of Macedonia, fleeing to Epirus with Alexander IV, the remaining king, and his mother Roxanna and grandmother Olympias. The latter had originally stayed purposely distant from the clash between Polyperchon and Cassander, but soon realized the latter was intent on replacing her grandson and establishing a new (Antipatrid) dynasty. This would ultimately mean death for any Argeads Cassander perceived as standing in his way.

The Macedonian soldiery, always loyal to the memory of Alexander, came to the same conclusion and vocally supported Olympias' return. Soon Polyperchon and Olympias invaded Macedon with a combined force of loyalists and Epirotes, successfully driving Cassander from power. Olympias then convinced any troops who remained loyal to Arrhidaeus and his wife Eurydice to side with the Argeads. The soldiers then handed the latter two into her custody. She promptly had them executed in October 317 BC.

However, Olympias then initiated a brutal proscription of Cassander's family and supporters, horrifying many of the Macedonian nobility who had never forgotten her Epirot origins. Suddenly the Antipatrid cause was given renewed momentum, and in 316 BC Cassander gathered an army and besieged Olympias in Pydna on the Thessalian coast. In the negotiations that followed, Cassander guaranteed the lives of Olympias, Alexander IV and Roxanna (the latter two being besieged with her). However, he quickly reneged on this regarding Olympias and ordered the army to kill her. When they refused, he instead gathered the families of the victims of her earlier proscriptions who stoned her to death. Cassander then denied her the usual rites of burial. He continued to reign as regent over Alexander IV until, in 309 BC, he felt secure enough to have him and his mother Roxanna murdered, extinguishing the Argead line forever. Finally, he proclaimed himself king in 305 BC, establishing the short-lived Antipatrid dynasty.

Third War of the Diadochi

Back in Asia, after the final demise of Eumenes, Antigonus now controlled nearly all of Anatolia and most of the eastern satrapies,

Polyperchon and Cassander alternately controlled Macedon and the majority of Greece, Lysimachus still controlled Thrace and had remained largely aloof from the early phases of the Wars of the Successors, and Ptolemy controlled Egypt, Cyrene, Cyprus and most of Syria.

Soon, however, many of Antigonus' Asian satraps began to question his dominant position, particularly Seleucus in Babylonia. With the support of Cassander (now ascendent in Macedon) and Lysimachus, the satraps now demanded he break up his newly acquired empire. Specifically, in 314 BC they demanded Antigonus cede control of Lycia and Cappadocia in Anatolia to Cassander (notably a long way from Macedon), Hellespontine Phrygia in Anatolia to Lysimachus, the remainder of Syria to Ptolemy, and finally to give Seleucus independent control of Babylonia. They also demanded he share his immense wealth evenly among them given he controlled all the treasuries Alexander had captured from Darius III across the breadth of the Achaemenid Persian Empire.

Antigonus' reply was typically blunt. Be ready for war. This initiated the Third War of the Diadochi, a conflict between Antigonus and Demetrius on one side, and Cassander, Lysimachus, Ptolemy and Seleucus on the other. At stake was the integrity of Alexander's empire, this being the final time there was a chance it might remain largely intact (if the Antigonids won).

The conflict began in the spring of 314 BC when Antigonus invaded Ptolemaic Syria, besieging Tyre. Cassander and Ptolemy then prompted the Carian satrap Asander to move against Antigonus' territories in Lycia, Lydia and Phrygia. Antigonus responded cannily, forcing Cassander to focus on the Macedonian homeland by sending his old friend and *strategos* Aristodemus of Miletus to the Peloponnese with 1,000 talents of silver to raise a mercenary army to fight Cassander in the north. Once there, Aristodemus allied himself with the usurped regent, Polyperchon, who still controlled territory in Greece. With the new front opened in Greece, Antigonus then sent another loyal *strategos*, his nephew Ptolemaeus, through Anatolia to the Hellespont with the aim of cutting Asander off from his Lysimachid and Antipatrid allies in Europe. Ptolemaeus' lightning strike was highly successful, securing the whole of northwestern Anatolia for Antigonus. He then trapped Asander in Caria, though he proved unable to drive his opponent from the satrapy. Antigonus now decided to campaign against Asander himself, leaving Demetrius in Syria.

This was Demetrius' first time in sole command of his own field army. Ptolemy and Seleucus (who had made his way westwards from Babylon) immediately saw the opportunity, with the Antigonid army now split in two. They invaded Syria from the south with an army of 18,000 foot and 4,000 cavalry, forcing Demetrius to recall his troops from winter quarters and gather them in Gaza. There Demetrius' advisors suggested he withdraw to avoid battle given his lack of experience compared to the two leading Diadochi, but he ignored them. Clearly feeling the need to prove himself a battle-leader in his own right, he deployed his forces ready for an engagement. His army included 2,900 lance-armed shock cavalry, 1,500 light infantry and 30 Indian war elephants under his own command on the left. The Antigonid phalanx of 11,000 was deployed in the centre, with 13 war elephants in front and light infantry ahead of them. On his right Demetrius deployed 1,500 lighter cavalry.

As Ptolemy and Seleucus arrived, they found Demetrius' army deployed and acted accordingly. Their original plan had been to put most of their cavalry on the left, but they now switched to mass their 3,000 best cavalry on the right, under their personal command. Additionally, they had earlier created an anti-elephant corps of 3,000 light infantry equipped with devices featuring spikes connected by chains. These were positioned in front of their right-wing cavalry with orders to throw them in the path of any beast which charged them, and to target their mahouts (drivers) with javelins. Their phalanx was stationed in the centre, with the remaining 1,000 cavalry deployed on the left.

The battle began with the two stronger cavalry wings driving back their foes. Here Demetrius was the more successful, forcing his opponents off the battlefield. However, though Ptolemy and Seleucus were less successful in comparison, they were cannier. Instead of pursuing, they swung around Demetrius's left to threaten the flank of the Antigonid phalanx.

Seeing this, Demetrius halted his pursuit and deployed the elephants on his right wing and centre. Here he hoped to demoralize the opposing phalanx. However, Ptolemy and Seleucus now deployed their anti-elephant troops across their whole frontage, with many beasts panicking when they stepped on the spiked chains. Many of their crews were then shot down by other light troops, with the Ptolemaic light infantry performing so well they captured numerous animals. The rest were killed.

The loss of his elephants badly affected the morale of Demetrius' cavalry, even those on his successful wing, and many retreated. Attention next turned to the phalanx battle which now began. Neither side could get the upper hand until the Antigonids noticed their cavalry beginning to waver. At that point their opponents got the upper hand, eventually forcing the Antigonids to surrender, who did so by raising their pikes. Demetrius was too preoccupied to intervene as he was rallying his cavalry. When he saw the battle was lost he withdrew his remaining troops, initially in good order, with Ptolemy and Seleucus pursuing. Notably, all three *strategos* had fought bravely in the front line like true Macedonian leaders.

The engagement had been a disaster for Demetrius, but worse was to follow. Romm explains the detail of what happened next:

> As the survivors retreated past Gaza, Demetrius' base of operations, some entered the city to retrieve the goods they had stored there. Demetrius knew this was no time to stop, but he could not prevent them. Their laden horses and mules clogged the gateways as they hurried out, each seeking not to be the last. Then, at the moment of

> greatest confusion, Ptolemy's pursuit troops arrived. The walls of Gaza could have kept them out, but the gates could not be closed in time with such a throng in the way. Ptolemy gained control of the fortified city, including the baggage train of Demetrius containing the young man's tent and personal effects.[1]

This was truly humiliating for Demetrius. Further, when he finally took a roll call of his survivors, he found he had lost 8,500 men. Of these 500 had died, mostly elite cavalry including his leading commander Pithon. The rest had surrendered, including most of his phalanx, who would now fight for Ptolemy. At a strategic level, the result was also devastating for the Antigonids. Ptolemy now absorbed their territory in the Levant, including the vital ports on the Mediterranean coast. Meanwhile, Seleucus headed back east to secure control of the eastern satrapies with 1,000 men provided by Ptolemy. There he established what later became the Seleucid Empire. All in all, an inauspicious start for Demetrius when commanding alone.

However, fortune then smiled on Demetrius. This was because Ptolemy was in a forgiving mood. He saw no reason to humiliate Antigonus' son further, playing a long game given he knew at some stage a peace would be agreed. The Egyptian ruler sent back all of Demetrius' captured Companion cavalry, together with the effects seized in his tent in Gaza. Plutarch says he also sent Demetrius a personal message, saying 'the war between you and me must not be over everything, but glory and sovereignty'.[2]

In effect, he wanted a strategic balance agreed between the Antigonids and Egypt. Demetrius replied with equal benevolence, thanking Ptolemy for the men and goods.

However, that wasn't the end of it. When Antigonus heard the news back in Celaenae he was furious. Not with his son, but with himself for not foreseeing Ptolemy's move. Plutarch provides the detail, saying:

> When Antigonus learned of the battle, he said that Ptolemy had conquered beardless youths, but must now fight with men; however, not wishing to humble or curtail the spirit of his son, he did not oppose his request that he might fight again on his own account, but suffered him to do it.[3]

With that, Demetrius set about rebuilding his army, and was soon back in the field. His rapprochement with Ptolemy was quickly over, a lengthy struggle now beginning. Plutarch again provides the detail, this time of the next engagement where Demetrius was far more successful, and happy to return Ptolemy's earlier chivalry:

> And not long after, up came Cilles, a general of Ptolemy, with a splendid army, intending to drive Demetrius out of all Syria, and looking down upon him because of his previous defeat. But Demetrius fell upon him suddenly and took him by surprise, put him to rout, and captured his camp, general and all; he also took 7,000 of his soldiers prisoner, and made himself master of vast treasures. However, he rejoiced to have won the day, not by reason of what he was going to have, but of what he could restore, and was delighted, not so much with the wealth and glory which his victory brought, as with the power it gave him to recompense the kindness and return the favour of Ptolemy. And yet he did not do this on his own responsibility, but first wrote to his father about it. And when his father gave him permission and bade him dispose of everything as he liked, he sent back to Ptolemy both Cilles himself and his friends, after loading them with gifts. This reverse drove Ptolemy out of Syria, and brought Antigonus down from Celaenae; he rejoiced at the victory and yearned to get sight of the son who had won it.[4]

While in the Levant with Demetrius, Antigonus delivered his famous 'Decree of the Macedonians' speech outside the city of Tyre. In the first instance this demanded Cassander hand over Alexander IV and

Roxanna into Antigonid protection, and also destroy Thebes and Olynthus where Antipatrid support was strong. However, the next part of the proclamation was aimed directly at the other Greek city-states and was to have huge ramifications for the governance of the *poleis* there for the next fifteen years, setting the tone for the future Antigonid and Antipadrid rivalry in the Balkans. Crucially, he declared that under him the city-states would be free and ungarrisoned, beyond any form of direct Macedonian control. In effect this was a return to the pre-Chaeronea status quo and set the democratic factions within each *polis* against any pro-Antipadrid oligarchs and tyrants being propped up by the existing Macedonian garrisons. To make sure that his words were spread far and wide, Antigonus distributed copies of the proclamation across the Hellenistic world, particularly in Greece. The 'Decree of the Macedonians' unleashed democratic fever across mainland Greece, with drastic consequences. In Argos, one of the first city-states to react, the democratic faction revolted and asked for Antigonid assistance. Cassander's men arrived first and burned 500 rebels alive after they'd gathered in their city hall. A spiral of bloody civil wars followed as, *polis* by *polis*, Antigonid democratic factions fought Antipadrid oligarchs and tyrants.

Back in Asia, Antigonus sent Demetrius east to pursue the ambitious Seleucus in a lightning campaign. His specific brief was to recover Babylonia, Seleucus' powerbase. Wheatley provides the detail, saying:

> At some time in late November or early December, Demetrius left Damascus at the head of a large army comprising 5,000 Macedonian and 10,000 mercenary foot, and 4,000 horse. He found that Seleucus was long gone, and Babylon evacuated, with only the two citadels (or palaces) defended. He promptly captured, plundered, and garrisoned one of them, but after trying for several days, realized that the second could not be reduced by his deadline. Demetrius encountered no other concerted opposition in the largely deserted satrapy, but was covertly

> monitored by the Seleucid general Patrocles, who supplied his master with detailed intelligence regarding enemy activities.[5]

Plutarch then says that, with the deadline set by his father approaching, Demetrius began a systematic devastation of Babylon and the surrounding countryside.[6]

He then returned to Antigonus with a vast amount of loot, leaving behind a garrison of 6,000 under the *strategos* Archelaus.[7] In the long run this would be counterproductive, given his destructive behaviour would turn the eastern satrapies away from the Antigonids and towards Seleucus. For now though, Antigonus had even more money to hire mercenaries.

Soon Demetrius was back in action in the west, with Diodorus Siculus saying he expelled the forces of Ptolemy from Cilicia Trachea. Ptolemy responded by sending his fleet to besiege Halicarnassus in south-western Anatolia.[8] Plutarch then has Demetrius quickly heading further west to relieve the city.[9]

By this point Antigonus decided the exhausting conflict against the other Successors should conclude. In short order, peace treaties were signed with Cassander, Lysimachus and Ptolemy, though he continued the war with Seleucus while attempting to recover his eastern satrapies. With peace settled in the west, in 310 BC Antigonus then headed east himself, though he was unable to defeat Seleucus and was forced to finally give up his former territories there.

It was Antigonus' focus in the east that gave Cassander the free hand he needed back in Macedon, allowing him to murder Alexander IV and Roxanna in 309 BC. The Third War of the Diadochi petered out around this time, leaving just five of Alexander's immediate successors still at large. These were Cassander, Lysimachus, Ptolemy, Seleucus (the true winner of this conflict) and Antigonus (together with Demetrius).

The Fourth War of the Diadochi

The stakes remained very high for all the protagonists across the Hellenistic world, and war again broke out around 307 BC. Emboldened by Antigonus' inability to defeat Seleucus, Ptolemy had by this time expanded his region of control in the eastern Mediterranean to include Cyprus and much of the Aegean. Meanwhile, in the east, Seleucus decided to carry out his own *anabasis*, aiming to secure control of his newly acquired eastern satrapies. Seeing his former opponents acting with impunity, Antigonus now realized he had to act or risk losing authority over his remaining territories.

His first target was Greece, the soft underbelly of Antipatrid Macedon, where he decided to send Demetrius on his first campaign there. Here, Antigonus aimed high. Not for him the Peloponnese, Aetolia or Euobea. Only Athens would do, the *polis* still far outshining its rivals despite declining fortunes. At this time, it was back in Cassander's control and a cornerstone of the latter's strategy to dominate all of Greece. The city was ruled by the tyrant Demetrius of Phalerum, a notable statesman set in place by Cassander. Athenaeus describes him as a man infamous for lavish feasts, affairs with youths and women, and a blatant narcissist who erected 360 statues in his own honour around the city.[10] In his favour, he was also a noted rhetorician, historian and legal reformer. Antigonus knew that seizing the city and its harbour Piraeus would provide the perfect strategic platform, giving him the choice of striking Cassander to the north or south, and by land or sea, thus keeping Antipatrid forces second-guessing his plans. The Decree of the Macedonians remained the centrepiece of Antigonid foreign policy in Greece, enabling Antigonus and Demetrius to portray themselves as champions of liberty for the *poleis*. Diodorus Siculus says that when he appointed Demetrius to lead the Antigonid campaign in Greece, Antigonus specifically gave him the order to 'free all the cities throughout Greece' and remove their Antipatrid garrisons.[11]

Already assured the support of the democrats in Athens, Antigonus and Demetrius settled on a very bold plan involving securing Piraeus in a lightning strike to diminish the authority of Demetrius of Phalerum. Antigonus gave his son 5,000 talents and a fleet of 250 ships for the campaign, this sailing from Ephesus to Cape Sounion (the southernmost point of Attica) in June 307 BC. On arrival, he then deployed a stratagem which completely wrong-footed his Athenian namesake. His ships safely assembled, Demetrius sailed twenty of his best vessels northwards towards the Corinthian port of Cenchreae.

Polyaenus says the Athenians fell for the bluff completely, standing down their guards as they assumed the ships belonged to their existing foe, Ptolemaeus.[12] Then, as soon as Demetrius received word of this, he changed course immediately and bolted for Piraeus, the oarsmen in his galleys rowing at maximum speed. They arrived unopposed, Demetrius telling the startled audience of dockworkers and locals from the bow of his war galley that he had arrived to set the Athenians free from tyranny and restore democratic government. He received a genuinely warm reception from the dockworkers, with Piraeus always a centre of democratic support, though the town itself kept its gates closed.

Encouraged by his immediate support on arrival on the dockside, Demetrius jumped ashore to begin his crusade to free the Greeks. He then unleashed his remaining ships and troops on Piraeus itself, its defence led by Demetrius of Phalerum in person, the latter clearly more than the dandy Athenaeus describes above. However, soon the town walls were breached and the remaining garrison fled, with the Athenian tyrant speeding back to Athens. There, having been duped by Demetrius and defeated, his position proved untenable, with Plutarch saying he was 'more afraid of his fellow citizens than of the enemy'.[13] He departed for Thebes under a guarantee of safe conduct, ultimately finding his way to Ptolemy's court in Alexandria, and later dying of a snakebite in the southern Egyptian desert.

Meanwhile, back in Athens the population was jubilant that their tyrant had been overthrown, destroying all but one of his statues and making their remains into chamber pots. Demetrius now focused on reducing the nearby fortress of Munychia which still held out against him. Using artillery and sappers to great effect, he opened a breach in its strong walls within two days. The garrison then surrendered. Demetrius next levelled the stronghold to remove this potent symbol of Antipatrid control. He entered Athens itself in triumph, restoring democratic government, with the leading democrat Stratocles taking charge. As a first act, the new Athenian assembly voted to set up gold-plated statues of Antigonus and Demetrius in a victory chariot. These were placed in the market square, next to two other statues of earlier liberators called the Tyrannicides. That was only the beginning, as Romm details:

> Gold wreaths of massive weight were awarded to both the Antigonids, and civic honours were heaped on their friends and relations. The epithet 'Saviours', a consecrated word, was conferred on both father and son as a kind of official title, and an altar was set up at which the populace could make an official sacrifice to 'the Saviour Gods'. The names Demetrius and Antigonus, in adjectival form, were plastered everywhere: on yearly athletic games, on months of the calendar year, with two Athenian tribes [newly established in their honour], and on two new 'sacred' *triremes*, ships reserved for ceremonial functions.[14]

Such were the extraordinary rewards for the victors. While some Athenians challenged such sycophancy, having only just seen off one oppressor, most accepted it as a price worth paying for keeping the hated Cassander out of their affairs. Antigonus, taken aback at such immediate success, responded warmly to the Athenian plaudits, gifting the city timber to build 100 ships, 6,000 tonnes of grain and giving back control of the island of Imbros in the northeastern Aegean. With the democrats back in power, notable exiles then began to return to Athens, including Zeno of Citium, the founder of stoicism. To cement his position as the saviour of Greek democracy, Demetrius then took a second wife, a high-born Athenian woman called Eurydice. The only jarring note during this period was the ruling council banning the founding of any new schools of philosophy in Athens without their consent.

Demetrius next moved on nearby Megara in western Attica, capturing it and expelling Cassander's garrison with apparent ease. Then, in a foreign policy twist, Antigonus decided to change the point of attack against his opponents. In the spring of 306 BC he ordered Demetrius to conquer Ptolemaic-controlled Cyprus. By this time, the Egyptian ruler had already installed garrisons of his own in Corinth to close off land access to the Peloponnese, and also in Sicyon southwest of Athens, and was using Cyprus to support these operations and to raid Anatolia. To reassure his new Antigonid allies in Greece, Demetrius called together counsellors from all the cities under their protection, with Plutarch saying he was reluctant to leave given he believed the war for the liberation of Greece was nobler than fighting Ptolemy in Cyprus.[15]

However, following his father's orders, Demetrius departed nevertheless, successfully storming the Cypriot port towns of Carpasia and Urania, and then investing the city of Salamis, the Ptolemaic capital of the island. Here he established a blockade on both land and sea, though not before Ptolemy's brother and the Cypriot governor Menelaus had sent messengers to Egypt requesting help.

Here Demetrius had a large store of catapults, stone-throwers and other siege machinery. However, knowing Ptolemaic reinforcements could arrive at any minute, he also sent to Greece for technicians to build the first of his legendary specialized siege towers. This was an eight-storey *helepolis* equipped with its own artillery, which together with two penthoused battering rams formed the centrepiece of his assault. At first the Salaminians put up a tough resistance. The *helepolis* and rams proved decisive though, clearing the battlements and reducing sections of the defensive wall circuit to rubble. With the city seeming about to fall, Demetrius prepared his final assault. However, Menelaus then launched a nighttime sortie which caught the Antigonids by surprise. He succeeded in setting the *helepolis* and other siege machinery alight. Demetrius was now forced to persevere without them, and soon a stalemate was reached. Then word reached him that Ptolemy was arriving with his fleet to relieve the city, forcing him to break off the siege and return to his ships at sea. What followed was one of the great naval battles of the ancient world, and arguably Demetrius' greatest military success. Diodorus Siculus provides a very detailed account of this engagement, which I record in full:

> At first, while it was still night, Ptolemy made for Salamis at top speed, believing that he could gain an entrance [to the harbour there] before the enemy was ready; but as day broke, the fleet of Demetrius in battle array was visible at no great distance, and Ptolemy also prepared for the battle. Ordering his supply ships to follow at a distance, he himself took command of the left wing with the largest of his warships fighting under him. After the fleet had been disposed in this way, both sides prayed to the gods as was the custom, the signalmen leading and the crews joining in the response. The two leaders, since they were about to fight for their lives and their all, were in much anxiety. When Demetrius was about three stades distant from the enemy, he raised the battle signal that had been agreed upon, a gilded shield, and this sign was made known to all by being repeated in relays. Since Ptolemy also gave a similar signal, the distance between the fleets was rapidly reduced. When the trumpets gave the signal for battle and both forces raised the battle cry, all the ships rushed to the encounter in a terrifying manner; using their bows and their ballistae at first, then their javelins in a shower, the men wounded those who were within range; then

when the ships had come close together and the encounter was about to take place with violence, the soldiers on the decks crouched down and the oarsmen, spurred on by the signalmen, bent more desperately to their oars. As the ships drove together with force and violence, in some cases they swept off each other's oars so that the ships became useless for flight or pursuit, and the men who were on board, though eager for a fight, were prevented from joining in the battle; but where the ships had met prow to prow with their rams, they drew back for another charge, and the soldiers on board shot at each other with effect since the mark was close at hand for each party. Some of the men, when their captains had delivered a broadside blow and the rams had become firmly fixed, leaped aboard the ships of the enemy, receiving and giving severe wounds; for certain of them, after grasping the rail of a ship that was drawing near, missed their footing, fell into the sea, and at once were killed with spears by those who stood above them; and others, making good their intent, slew some of the enemy and, forcing others along the narrow deck, drove them into the sea. As a whole the fighting was varied and full of surprises: many times those who were weaker got the upper hand because of the height of their ships, and those who were stronger were foiled by inferiority of position and by the irregularity with which things happen in fighting of this kind. For in contests on land, valour is made clearly evident, since it is able to gain the upper hand when nothing external and fortuitous interferes; but in naval battles there are many causes of various kinds that, contrary to reason, defeat those who would properly gain the victory through prowess. Demetrius fought most brilliantly of all, having taken his stand on the stern of his seven. A crowd of men rushed upon him, but by hurling his javelins at some of them and by striking others at close range with his spear, he slew them; and although many missiles of all sorts were aimed at him, he avoided some that he saw in time and received others upon his defensive armour. Of the three men who protected him with shields, one fell struck by a lance and the other two were severely wounded. Finally Demetrius drove back the forces confronting him, created a rout in the right wing, and forthwith forced even the ships next to the wing to flee. Ptolemy who had with

> himself the heaviest of his ships and the strongest men, easily routed those stationed opposite him, sinking some of the ships and capturing others with their crews. Turning back from that victorious action, he expected to easily subdue the others also; but when he saw that the right wing of his forces had been shattered and all those next to that wing driven into flight, and further, that Demetrius was pressing on with full force, he sailed back to Citium [in southern Cyprus].[16]

This stunning victory finally decided the outcome of the campaign, with Menelaus soon surrendering the island. It later became the centre of Demetrius' military operations in the eastern Mediterranean. However, his first act now was to send messengers to his father with the good news. They found him in Syria where he was constructing his new capital city, Antigoneia-on-the-Orontes. When he heard of his son's fabulous victory, Antigonus triggered what was clearly a long-planned coronation, with the crowds acclaiming him king and producing a diadem which his leading officers set on his head. This was a simple monarchic headband as worn by Alexander. The message here was clear and simple. Antigonus was now a king, and Alexander's true heir. He also declared Demetrius a king, and his appointed successor. He then sent a similar diadem to his son. What territory they were kings of is unclear, given Seleucus held the eastern satrapies, Ptolemy Egypt, Lysimachus Thrace and Cassander Macedon itself. Nevertheless, as Romm says, seventeen years after the death of Alexander, and four year's after the extinction of the Argead line, the Hellenistic world had a viable royal family again.[17]

Building on his son's mighty success, and their regal anointing, Antigonus now led a large army against Egypt itself in late 306 BC. However, bad weather prevented Demetrius supplying him by sea and Antigonus was forced to withdraw. The two then considered their next move, alighting on another key island in the region as their target. This was Rhodes, the mercantile *polis* which controlled access to the Aegean with its large fleet. Traditionally Rhodes had remained neutral in regional conflicts given its entrepreneurial status. However, the Antigonids worried it was now edging into the Ptolemaic sphere of influence. After diplomatic outreach failed to confirm ongoing neutrality, the Antigonids initiated a large-scale invasion. Once more Demetrius was tasked with leading the campaign.

Demetrius' army totalled 40,000 men, with his fleet numbering 200 polyreme war galleys and 150 merchant vessels. He also enlisted many regional pirate fleets to assist the operation, with over 1,000 additional vessels joining his fleet. He gathered the vast armada at Loryma on the Carian mainland, directly opposite Rhodes city, ready to launch his assault (Bennett and Roberts, 2008, 143). Meanwhile, the Rhodians were able to muster a force of 6,000 citizens soldiers. They also manumitted thousands of slaves, who they promised to buy land for if they fought with their former masters.

Rhodes was the pinnacle of Demetrius' siege undertakings, where he used all of his experience to that point, most recently at Salamis. It was also the origin of the sobriquet by which he is known today, Poliorcetes, given it turned into an epic struggle lasting a whole year that captured the imagination of the entire Greek-speaking world.

He arrived off Rhodes in the summer of 305 BC to find the city and its main harbour strongly fortified. Note there is often controversy over the timeline of this siege; what you read here is my own reconstruction. Demetrius immediately imposed a naval blockade, but because of the layout of the harbour it proved impossible to stop Ptolemaic blockade runners breaking through. Therefore, securing the harbour became his first objective. At first he built his own port alongside the existing one. From this he then constructed a mole of rock and earth, then deploying a floating boom from this across the mouth of the Rhodian harbour. However, every night the defenders sallied out to cast it adrift.

It soon became apparent that a land campaign would be needed, and the Antigonid army now went ashore to prepare for a lengthy siege. Their first task was to build a huge, defended camp just out of missile range of the city, before ravaging the surrounding countryside to provide provisions, and also wood to build siege machinery. Here Diodorus Siculus is again our main source, with a very detailed account of the preparations for the land siege. He says:

> Demetrius, failing in his assaults by sea, decided to make his attacks by land. Having gathered a large quantity of material of all kinds, he built an engine called the *helepolis* [his second, after that at Salamis], which far surpassed in size those which had been constructed before it. Each side of the square platform he made almost 50 cubits in length, framed together from squared timber and fastened with iron; the space within he divided by bars set a cubit from each other so that there might be standing space for those who were to push the machine forward. The whole structure was movable, mounted on eight great solid wheels; the width of their rims was two cubits and these were overlaid with heavy iron plates. To permit motion to the side, pivots had been constructed, by means of which the whole device was easily moved in any direction. From each corner there extended upward beams equal in length and little short of 100 cubits long, inclining toward each other in such a way that, the whole structure being nine storeys high, the first storey had an area of 4,300 square feet and the topmost 900 square feet. The three exposed sides of the machine he covered externally with iron plates nailed on so that it should receive no injury from fire carriers. On each storey there were ports on the front, in size and shape fitted to the individual characteristics of the missiles that were to be shot forth. These ports had shutters, which were lifted by a mechanical device, and secured the safety of the men on the platforms who were busy serving the artillery; for the shutters were of hides stitched together and were filled with wool so that they would yield to the blows of the stones from the ballistae. Each of the storeys had two wide stairways, one of which they used for bringing

up what was needed and the other for descending, in order that all might be taken care of without confusion. Those who were to move the machine were selected from the whole army, 3,400 men excelling in strength; some of them were enclosed within the machine while others were stationed in its rear, and they pushed it forward, the skilful design aiding greatly in its motion. Demetrius also constructed penthouses, some to protect the men who were filling the moat, others to carry rams, and also covered passages through which those who were going to their labours might go and return safely. Using the crews of the ships, he cleared a space 4 stades wide through which he planned to advance the siege engines he had prepared, wide enough so that it covered a front of six curtain walls and seven towers. The number of craftsmen and labourers collected was not much less than 30,000.[18]

When all was ready Demetrius launched a devasting full-on assault against the city walls. These received a fearsome battering, with a huge defensive tower and a section of adjoining curtain wall reduced to ruin. However, when all seemed ready for his final assault through the breach, a diplomatic delegation arrived from the nearby Ionian Greek city of Knidos. Knowing the damage the destruction of Rhodes would do to the regional economy, they asked for time to convince the Rhodians to surrender. Demetrius had no choice but to agree, knowing much of the Greek-speaking world was already rooting for the plucky Rhodians. Even if he won a mighty victory, that last thing the Antigonids wanted was a public relations disaster. Sadly, the embassy failed, and Demetrius once more renewed his assault. However, to his evident surprise, the Rhodians had used the brief ceasefire to great effect. Diodorus Siculus again picks up the story:

When the Rhodians saw the progress of the enemy's siege works, they built a second wall inside, parallel to the one that was failing under the attacks. They used stones obtained by tearing down the theatre's outer wall and the adjacent houses, and also some of the temples, vowing

> to the Gods that they would build finer ones when the city had been saved. They also sent out nine of their ships, giving the commanders orders to sail in every direction and, appearing unexpectedly, to sink some of the ships they intercepted and bring others to the city. After these had sailed out they were divided into three groups. The *strategos* Damophilus sailed to Carpathos; and finding there many of Demetrius' ships, he sank some, shattering them with his rams, and some he beached and burnt after selecting the most useful men from their crews, and not a few of those that were transporting the grain from the island, he brought back to Rhodes. Another *strategos* called Menedemus, who commanded three light undecked ships, sailed to Patara in Lycia; and finding at anchor there a ship whose crew was on shore, he set the hull on fire; and he took many of the freighters that were carrying provisions for Demetrius' army and dispatched them to Rhodes. He also captured a quadrireme that was sailing from Cilicia and had on board royal robes and the rest of the outfit that Demetrius' wife Phila had with great pains made ready and sent off for her husband. This clothing Damophilus sent to Egypt since the garments were purple and proper for a king to wear; but the ship he hauled up on land, and he sold the sailors, both those from the quadrireme and those from the other captured ships. Finally the *strategos* Amyntas, who was in command of the three remaining ships, made for islands where he fell in with many freighters carrying to the enemy materials useful for the engines of war; he sank some of these and some he brought to the city. On these ships were also captured eleven famous engineers, men of outstanding skill in making missiles and catapults.[19]

This was commerce raiding of the finest order and proved a severe thorn in the side of Demetrius as he struggled to reduce the Rhodian defences. His offensive was then further disrupted by foul weather as the campaigning season neared its end. The Rhodians used this good fortune to launch a highly successful counterattack which captured the Antigonid garrison on the mole that Demetrius had constructed. By this point he had switched tactics to confuse the Rhodians, hoping to capture the city using tunnels dug by his sappers while the defenders remained fixated on his war machines. This also proved problematic. Again Diodorus Siculus has the detail:

> When Demetrius was undermining the wall by using his sappers, one of the deserters informed the besieged that those who were working underground were almost within the walls. Therefore, the Rhodians by digging a deep trench parallel to the wall which was expected to collapse and by quickly undertaking mining operations themselves, made contact with their opponents underground and prevented them from advancing farther. Now the mines were closely watched by both sides, and some of Demetrius' men tried to bribe Athenagoras, who had been given command of the guard by the Rhodians. This man was a Milesian by descent, sent by Ptolemy as commander of the mercenaries. Promising to turn traitor he set a day on which one of the ranking leaders should be sent from Demetrius to go by night through the mine up into the city in order to inspect the position where the soldiers would assemble. But after leading Demetrius on to great hopes, he disclosed the matter to the council; and when Demetrius sent one of his friends, Alexander the Macedonian, the Rhodians captured him as he came up through the mine. They crowned Athenagoras with a golden crown and gave him a gift of five talents of silver, their object being to stimulate loyalty to the city on the part of the other men who were mercenaries and foreigners.[20]

So ended the campaigning season of 305 BC, a frustrating one for Demetrius. He knew his attempts to reduce Rhodes were being watched closely by all the remaining Successors and their supporters, not least his father. He also knew he had to strike a balance, of needing to win the conflict as early as possible so as not to lose face, while not devasting Rhodes itself and alienating both existing Antigonid supporters and those still to choose a side in the war. He needed a swift victory, and the following April threw everything he had against the Rhodian defences. Once more, Diodorus Siculus provides the detail:

> Demetrius, when his engines of war were ready and all the space before the walls was cleared, stationed the *helepolis* in the centre, and assigned positions to the penthouses, eight in number, which were to protect the sappers. He placed four of these on each side of the *helepolis* and connected with each of them one covered passage so that the men who were going in and out might accomplish their assigned tasks in safety; and he brought up also two enormous penthouses in which battering rams were mounted. For each shed held a ram with a length of 120 cubits, sheathed with iron and striking a blow like that of a ship's ram; and the ram was moved with ease, being mounted on wheels and receiving its motive power in battle from not less than 1,000 men. When he was ready to advance the engines against the walls, he again placed on each storey of the *helepolis* ballistae and catapults of appropriate size, stationed his fleet in position to attack the harbours and the adjacent area, and distributed his infantry along such parts of the wall as could be attacked. Then, when all at a single command and signal had raised the battle cry together, he launched attacks on the city from every side.[21]

Sadly for Demetrius, when news of this savage onslaught reached Ptolemy and Cassander, they immediately acted to prevent Rhodes falling to the Antigonids. The former sent a large convoy of supply ships carrying reinforcements, weapons and food which Demetrius tried but failed to intercept. The vessels were soon inside the harbour in Rhodes. Meanwhile Cassander sent a similar relief force which also evaded the Antigonid fleet. Seeing this, Lysimachus also joined in, sending a convoy which also reached the harbour. Clearly Demetrius had lost control of the open ocean, with his naval forces spread too thinly. Emboldened, the Rhodian's now sallied out against Demetrius' siege works. Diodorus Siculus picks up the story again:

> Deciding that it would be advantageous to attack the siege engines of the enemy, they made ready a large supply of fire-bearing missiles and placed all their ballistae and catapults upon the wall. When night had fallen, at about the second watch, they suddenly began to strike the *helepolis* with an unremitting shower of the fire missiles, and by using other missiles of all kinds, they shot down any who rushed to the spot. Since the attack was unforeseen, Demetrius, alarmed for the siege works that had been constructed, hurried to the rescue. The night was moonless; and the fire missiles shone bright as they hurtled violently through the air; but the catapults and ballistae, since their missiles were invisible, destroyed many who were not able to see the impending stroke. It also happened that some of the iron plates of the *helepolis* were dislodged, and where the place was laid bare the fire missiles rained upon the exposed wood of the structure. Therefore Demetrius, fearing that the fire would spread and the whole machine be ruined, came quickly to the rescue, and with the water that had been placed in readiness on the platforms he tried to put out the spreading fire. He finally assembled by a trumpet signal the men who were assigned to move the apparatus and by their efforts dragged the machine beyond range. Then when day had dawned he ordered the camp followers to collect the missiles that had been hurled by the Rhodians, since he wished to estimate from these the armament of the forces within the city. Quickly carrying out his orders, they counted more than eight hundred fire missiles of various sizes and not less than 1,500 catapult bolts. Since so many missiles had been hurled in a short time at night, he marvelled at the resources possessed by the city and at their prodigality in the use of these weapons.[22]

Demetrius was a resilient leader and showed it here, quickly repairing the damaged engines. He was soon setting about the city walls again, knowing time might be running out for him. In short order another breach was made, and he readied his troops for a nighttime assault. Diodorus Siculus says that:

> Demetrius selected the strongest of his fighting men and of the rest those fitted for his purpose to the number of 1,500. These he ordered to advance to the wall in silence during the second watch; as for himself, when he had made his preparations, he gave orders to those stationed on each side that when he gave the signal they should raise the battle cry and make attacks both by land and sea. When they all carried out the order, those who had advanced against breaches in the walls, after dispatching the advance guards at the moat, charged past into the city and occupied the region of the theatre; but the magistrates of the Rhodians, learning what had happened and seeing that the whole city had been thrown into confusion, sent orders to those at the harbour and the walls to remain at their own posts and oppose the enemy outside if he should attack; and they themselves, with their contingent of selected men and the soldiers who had recently sailed in from Alexandria, attacked the troops who had got within the walls. When day returned and Demetrius raised the ensign, those who were attacking the port and those who had been stationed about the while on all sides shouted the battle cry, giving encouragement to the men who had occupied part of the region of the theatre; but in the city the throng of children and women were in fear and tears, thinking that their native city was being taken by storm. Nevertheless, fighting began between those who had made their way within the wall and the Rhodians, and many fell on both sides. At first neither side withdrew from its position; but afterwards, as the Rhodians constantly added to their numbers and were prompt to face danger, as is the way with men fighting for their native land and their most precious things, things turned against the king's men. Alcimus and Mantias, their commanders, expired after receiving many wounds, most of the others were killed in hand-to-hand fighting or were captured, and only a few escaped to Demetrius and survived. Many also of the Rhodians were slain, among whom was the president Damoteles, who had won great acclaim for his valour.[23]

Even after this latest setback Demetrius planned another assault. However, sadly for him, time really had run out. That was because

Antigonus had tired of the sanguinary and costly siege. Instead, he ordered Demetrius to make terms with the Rhodians and head back to Greece where the Antigonids were facing a new crisis.

Demetrius has often been criticized for his failure to capture Rhodes, though clearly other factors were in play, including the Antigonid reputation in the Greek speaking world. No doubt in the long run Demetrius would have been successful, if at great cost, and here Antigonus clearly chose to cut his losses.

In addition to the brave Rhodians, the other winners here were Ptolemy, Cassander and Lysimachus who were voted honours by the Rhodians, with statues constructed in their honour. Shortly after, Ptolemy was deified, with a temple constructed in his name in the Rhodian agora. Meanwhile, Demetrius' *helepolis* and other siege machinery had been abandoned after the Antigonids left. Several years later the former's metal plates and fittings, and those of the other engines, were melted down by the Rhodians. They used this, and the money they raised from selling the other remains of the engines, to erect an enormous statue of their sun-God Helios towering over their harbour. One of the seven wonders of the ancient world, this remains famous to this day as the Colossus of Rhodes, though it has long since vanished.

After disentangling himself from Rhodes, Demetrius sailed with 330 ships through the Aegean and landed at Aulis in Boeotia in August 304 BC. In the wider peninsula, Athens remained the centre of Antigonid support. For example, an Athenian inscription from this period records a donation of 140 talents of silver from Antigonus, while another thanks the friends of Demetrius for 'sharing the struggle for freedom and democracy'. The conflict in Greece had spluttered on while Demetrius was preoccupied with Rhodes, with the Athenians winning some early victories against Cassander until the now-king of Macedon directed his full attention south again. The Antigonids then lost the initiative, with the Antipatrids gaining fresh momentum. The Macedonians then attacked Athens directly, capturing the border forts that guarded the passes between Boeotia in Central Greece and the city, and then taking it under siege. By the summer of 304 BC, as Demetrius was wrapping things up in Rhodes, the situation in Athens had become desperate.

While still smarting from his failure in Rhodes, Demetrius was more than happy to renew his conflict with the regicide Cassander in person. He immediately set about attacking the Macedonian king's allies in Beoetia, taking Chalcis and expelling its Macedonian garrison. Given this was to the rear of Cassander's army assaulting Athens, the Macedonian king was forced to call off his attack there. Demetrius lost no time, quickly reforming the Antigonid alliance with the Boeotians and the Aetolians. This secured Central Greece for them, trapping Cassander's army. He then mounted one of his characteristic lightning strikes, targeting the Antipatrid forces withdrawing from their siege of Athens. Cassander, knowing he was cut off by land, fled back to Macedon by sea with as much of his army as his ships could carry. The Antigonids pursued all the way, their land forces also driving north. Soon the latter had captured Heraclea in Trachis on the southern border of Thessaly. There 6,000 Macedonians deserted and joined Demetrius, a significant number given it amounted to one fifth of the entire 'home army' at the time.

Then, at the beginning of the 303 BC campaigning season, Demetrius switched his point of attack to head south. Here he led a stunning campaign, his aim to draw Cassander into a meeting engagement where, if successful, he could remove him from the throne and add Macedonia to the Antigonid empire. There is no indication that Demetrius wanted to be the king of Macedon at this stage, he remaining truly loyal to his father.

His first target was Corinth, one of the 'fetters of Greece'. The Besieger landed at Cenchreae in the eastern Peloponnese. Once this was secure, he headed inland, bypassing Corinth to strike Sicyon on the north coast. This was still held by Ptolemy's garrison, and was his last foothold in Greece. Demetrius stormed the city's walls in a night attack and drove the defenders into the citadel where they soon surrendered and returned to Egypt. The grateful citizens then outdid Athens in their thanks to the Antigonids, renaming the city Demetrias in his honour. He then moved on to Corinth, where his democratic supporters opened a gate allowing his forces to take the city unopposed. The Antipatrid garrison then retreated to man the Acrocorinth citadel towering over the city, and the Aisyphium fort on its lower slopes. Demetrius lived up to his Poliorcetes nickname, deploying his siege engines to soften up the defences of the citadel and fort before storming the latter. This quickly fell, with the Macedonian troops atop the citadel surrendering soon after. Impressed, the Athenians responded to these victories by voting for annual sacrifices to Athena, Nike and Fortune, and to their saviours Antigonus and Demetrius.

Demetrius' campaign continued into the summer, next invading the Argolid Peninsula in the north-western Peloponnese. In short order he took the cities of Troezen, Epidaurus and Argos where, in June, he then presided over the festival of Hera. He also took a third wife called Deidameia, the sister of the 16-year-old exiled Epirot king Pyrrhus. This was a shrewd diplomatic move given the latter had been removed from his throne by allies of Cassander.

Demetrius' continued his lightning campaign, storming a number of towns in the northwestern Peloponnese before arriving at Orchomenus. Here, the Antipatrid garrison was commanded by a *strategos* called Strombichus, originally appointed under Polyperchon. The Besieger again lived up to his name and the city fell, with the 2,000 strong garrison joining the Antigonids. Strombichus wasn't so lucky, he and eight other officers being crucified. Such brutality, not uncommon in this Antigonid and Antipatrid fight to the death in Greece, had the desired effect and from that point until the end of the campaign, every time Demetrius approached a city with his 'great army and with overwhelming engines of war', the garrison surrendered immediately.[24] Demetrius then returned to Athens to spend the winter, content in the knowledge that in just two campaigning seasons he had effectively destroyed Cassander's hold on mainland Greece.

Sadly for the Antigonids, Demetrius now displayed the more debauched side of his personality. He personally acquired the rear chamber of the Parthenon atop the Acropolis in Athens as his living quarters, where he set up his prize collection of courtesans under the command of an ageing madam called Lamia. From there he spent the winter months in a wild round of parties and orgies. One of the more salacious tales of this time has him courting a young boy named Democles the Handsome. When the youth kept on refusing his attentions he cornered him at the public baths. Having no way of escape, the proud Democles took the lid off the hot water cauldron there and jumped in, killing himself. Demetrius also demanded 250 silver talents from the Athenian assembly, his aim to give it to Lamia and the other courtesans to buy soap and cosmetics. Additionally, he had coins struck featuring his image on one side and Athena on the other. However, he overstepped the mark when he intervened personally in a legal case. Here the Athenian assembly acted against him for the first time, forbidding him from doing so again, but reversed the decision when he lost his temper with them. His critics in the city said this was far from the freedom they had been promised, though he lost no time in reminding them that such was the cost of keeping the Antipatrids out of Athenian affairs.

In 302 BC, Demetrius and his father resurrected Philip II's old League of Corinth, Demetrius henceforth acting as its commander. Cassander knew by this point that he was beaten, and sent envoys to Antigonus. However, the latter was in no mood to compromise and the Macedonian king's terms were rejected out of hand. Cassander then panicked and renewed his offensive against the Antigonids, aware he was beginning to appear weak to the unforgiving Macedonian aristocracy. For support he turned in desperation to Lysimchus, then campaigning against Antigonus in Caria. Here the Antipadrid king hoped to distract Antigonus' attention away from matters in Greece, sending his *strategos* Prepelaus with a small army to aid the Thraco-Macedonian king.

Back in Europe the war ground on, with Cassander aggressive once more while his ally Lysimachus continued to press Antigonus in Caria. With the remaining troops of the 'home army', Cassander then marched through Thessaly and occupied the passes controlling access to the south. Demetrius countered with typical rapidity, gathering his army and fleet at Chalcis and sailing from there to the port of Larisa Cremaste, north of the pass of Thermopylae. There he quickly took the city, disembarked his full force and marched north into Thessaly where he captured more cities. Cassander decided to make a stand at Pherae in southeastern Thessaly, where he strengthened the garrison and deployed his full field army, by now comprising 29,000 foot (including many mercenaries) and 2,000 cavalry. Demetrius could deploy 56,000 foot and 1,500 cavalry, an enormous army for the period. The Antipadrid king was no fool and wisely decided to remain in his nearby fortified camp, where the two sides faced off against each other for two weeks. Demetrius used the time well, convincing the citizens of Pherae to surrender the city, the garrison also capitulating on good terms.

It was at this moment of dramatic impasse, with Demetrius seemingly poised to make his killer blow against Cassander and seize the Macedonian throne for the Antigonids, that the wheels of fate again spun, and this time against him. For it was now that Antigonus, on the back foot against Lysimachus, dramatically recalled Demetrius to join him. The Antigonid heir swiftly came to terms with Cassander, once more reassuring the Greeks he would return as soon as fortune permitted, and then left with his fleet and much of the army for a date with destiny few could have foreseen.

On arrival in Caria, Demetrius found his ageing father in trouble. By this time Lysimachus had overrun much of western Anatolia, and although Demetrius strove to turn things around for Antigonus, by 301 BC the forces of Lysimachus and Cassander (not there in person, but happy to supply troops) had isolated them near Ipsus in Phrygia. The Antigonids now went on the offensive one last time, their combined forces finally driving back their opponents in a short campaign. Then, just as the Antigonids were poised for victory, Seleucus suddenly appeared from the east with his son Antiochus and a large army of reinforcements (many supplied by Ptolemy) to support Lysimachus. The latter now forced a decisive meeting engagement, this a true battle of the five armies, and one of the last of the Successor wars. Here the Antigonids fielded 70,000 foot, 10,000 cavalry and 75 elephants against the combined armies of Lysimachus, Cassander and Seleucus with 64,000 foot, 15,000 cavalry (many arriving from the east with Seleucus), 400 elephants and 100 scythed chariots.

The Battle of Ipsus opened with Demetrius charging at the head of the Antigonid right-wing cavalry against Antiochus who commanded the allied left wing. Demetrius' assault shattered all before him and soon the entire allied left had been driven from the field. Plutarch has him fighting brilliantly.[25] However, instead of halting his pursuit in true Alexandrian fashion and then turning this huge success to the advantage of the wider army, his exuberant troops pursued their routing opponents far from the battlefield. Meanwhile, Antigonus' phalanx charged the allied heavy foot and started to make good headway. However, given the lack of any cavalry from either side now on the Antigonid right and allied left, both phalanx flanks there were completely exposed. It was Seleucus who was the first to react. Gathering a reserve of allied cavalry, he now moved to threaten the exposed right flank of Antigonus' phalanx, with the pikemen there quickly surrendering en masse. This put the wider Antigonid cause in great peril, Antigonus sending messenger after messenger to demand his son return. However, when at last Demetrius did respond he was too late as the canny Seleucus had deployed a line of elephants on the allied left to prevent his return. The 81-year-old Antigonus, isolated, fought to the last, dying bravely with his guard phalangites while still awaiting the return of his wayward son. So ended the last attempt to reunite the empire of Alexander, with the surviving Successors now adopting the paraphernalia of monarchy in their own territories and turning their backs on the all-encompassing ambitions of the former great conqueror. And now, for the first time, Demetrius was alone as Antigonid leader, without his beloved father to guide him.

Chapter 5

Demetrius: Heir to Alexander

Each successor kingdom now went their own way, dealing with foreign policy and domestic issues in isolation rather than acting collectively. Most military engagements over the next decade took place in the context of the future of the Macedonian throne, and usually involved Demetrius, whose personal ambition was now even greater following the death of his father. What followed was a remarkable Errol Flynn-like existence of Hellenistic derring-do which lasted almost two decades.

Fallout From Ipsus

Demetrius never retrieved his father's body, with Seleucus' elephants forming an impenetrable barrier. Riddled with javelins, the corpse lay in the dusty plain for hours, attended only by the one retainer brave enough to remain as the Antigonid army routed. This was Thorax of Larissa, a long-term friend. We have no detail of the fate of the body, though some have speculated that the Belevi Mausoleum built 14km north of Ephesus may have been his intended burial place, even if it wasn't used for the purpose. This was the second largest mausoleum in Anatolia after that at Halicarnassus and would certainly have been a fitting respecting place for this giant among the Diadochi.

What of Demetrius? No doubt with a last, heartbreaking look back to where his father lay, he fled. The weight of grief and guilt would have broken a lesser man. In one roll of the dice the Antigonids had lost their senior king and empire, which the delighted Lysimachus,

Cassander and Seleucus started carving up, no doubt with Ptolemy joining in too. Demetrius was now at the bottom rung of the wheel of fortune.[1]

However, once more he proved incredibly resilient. Gathering the surviving horse from his unbroken wing at Ipsus, together with any surviving foot who could escape the pursuing allies, he fled for Ephesus where he eventually gathered a force of 4,000 cavalry and 5,000 foot. There he assessed the situation. He still had control of his fleet, one of the largest in the eastern Mediterranean, while territorially the Aegean islands and Cyprus also remained loyal. They would form the core of what would later become an island empire. Athens was also still nominally loyal to him (more of that later), as was Corinth. However, he needed money to pay his troops and sailors, but had none. Resisting urges to plunder the fabulously rich temples in Ephesus, instead he boarded ship and sailed east to Cilicia where he knew his father's treasuries were still intact. While there he also evacuated his wife Phila, his children by her, and his mother Stratonice. By this time the region had been given to Cassander's brother Pleistarchus as part of the post-Ipsus settlement. He had yet to arrive though, and Demetrius was able to relocate both the treasure and his family to Cyprus. Keenly aware of the public relations implications of the disaster at Ipsus, he also began issuing a new range of coins depicting himself on one side and Poseidon the other. This told the world the Antigonids were not finished, and to look to the seas. So it proved.

However, before he could go back on the offensive, he received more bad news. He decided Athens would be his next priority given a large part of his fleet was still there, as was his third wife Deidameia. Leaving the evacuated family behind in Cyprus, he headed for Attica. Plutarch picks up the story with his usual thoroughness:

> Demetrius thought that in his evil plight no refuge could be more secure than the goodwill of Athens. Therefore when, as he drew near the Cyclades islands, an embassy from Athens met him with a request to keep away from the city, on the grounds that the people had passed a vote to admit none of the kings, and informing him that Deidameia had been sent to Megara with fitting escort and honour, his wrath drove him beyond all proper bounds, although he had borne his other misfortunes very easily, and in so great a reversal of his situation had shown himself neither mean-spirited nor ignoble. But that the Athenians should disappoint his hopes and play him false, and that their apparent goodwill should prove on trial to be false and empty, was painful to him...Demetrius thought himself grievously wronged; but since he was unable to avenge himself, he sent a message to the Athenians in which he mildly expostulated with them, and asked that his ships be given back to him, among which was also the one having thirteen banks of oars. These he obtained, and then coasted along to the Isthmus, where he found his affairs in a very sorry state. For his garrisons were everywhere being expelled, and there was a general defection to his enemies. He therefore left Pyrrhus [Deidameia's brother and still the exiled Epirot king] in charge of Greece, while he himself put to sea and sailed to the Chersonesus.[2]

What Demetrius needed was a win, and quickly. With his fleet restored to full strength, soon it was payback time for Lysimachus, the Successor who had led his father's downfall at Ipsus. Plutarch continues his narrative, saying:

> Here he ravaged the territory of Lysimachus, thereby enriching and holding together his own forces, which were beginning to recover their spirit and to show themselves formidable again. Nor did the other kings try to help Lysimachus; they thought that he was no less objectionable than Demetrius, and that because he had more power he was even more to be feared.[3]

Demetrius' strategy was to launch a series of naval hit and run raids up and down the Thracian Chersoneses, today called the Gallipoli Peninsula. Here he struck some of the key Greek-speaking cities in a campaign that ran for a year from 300 BC. The settlements there were fabulously wealthy as they sat at the crucial maritime crossroads between the Black Sea and eastern Mediterranean. Soon his coffers were overflowing again, and his troops and sailors well paid and well fed. Additionally, targeting Lysimachus first was politically astute.

This was the Diadochus who had inherited most of the Antigonid empire. Furthermore, he was the most isolated with his core territories in Thrace, and also the most dangerous to his peers given he'd stayed aloof from the earlier rounds of the Successor wars.

In this campaign Demetrius was able to cross the Hellespont numerous times, at one point transporting 40,000 men. He captured the key city of Lampsacus twice and won numerous small engagements with Lysimachid troops. Yet his main aim here, in addition to looting Lysimachid cities, was to play a waiting game to see which of the victorious Diadochi would fall out first. It didn't take long. In 298 BC the all-powerful Ptolemy split with Seleucus and signed a formal alliance with Lysimachus. No doubt the latter thought Ptolemy's fleet would save the Chersonese from the attentions of Demetrius, but it had the opposite effect. That was because Seleucus, well placed to control the supply of Indian elephants to the Hellenistic world, now needed a new ally himself. He chose Demetrius.

What followed was a remarkable rehabilitation for the last surviving Antigonid ruler. Again, Plutarch gives a detailed account. He says:

> Not long afterwards Seleucus sent and asked the hand of Stratonicé, the daughter of Demetrius and Phila, in marriage. He had already, by Apama the Persian, a son Antiochus; but he thought that his realms would suffice for more successors than one, and that he needed this

> alliance with Demetrius, since he saw Lysimachus also taking one of Ptolemy's daughters for himself, and another for Agathocles his son. Now, to Demetrius, a marriage alliance with Seleucus was an unexpected piece of good fortune. So he took his daughter and sailed with his whole fleet to Syria. He was obliged to touch down at several places along the coast, and made landings in Cilicia, which country had been allotted by the victors at Ipsus to Pleistarchus, Cassander's brother. The latter was outraged by the arrival of Demetrius, and he wished to upbraid Seleucus for making an alliance with the common enemy independently of the other kings. So he went up to see him, leaving his territory unguarded. On learning of this, Demetrius set out from the seacoast for the Cilician city of Quinda; and finding 1,200 talents of its treasure still left, he packed them up, got them safely on-board ship, and put to sea with all speed. His wife Phila was already with him, and at Rhosus he was met by Seleucus. Their intercourse was at once put on a royal footing, and knew neither guile nor suspicion. First, Seleucus entertained Demetrius at his tent in the camp, then Demetrius in his turn received Seleucus on board the ship with thirteen banks of oars. There were also amusements, long conferences with one another and whole days spent together, all without guards or arms; until at length Seleucus took Stratonicé and went up in great state to Antioch. But Demetrius took possession of Cilicia, and sent Phila his wife to Cassander, who was her brother, that she might bring to naught the denunciations of Pleistarchus. In the meantime, Deidameia came by sea from Greece to join Demetrius, and after being with him a short time, succumbed to some disease. Then, by the intervention of Seleucus, friendship was made between Demetrius and Ptolemy, and it was agreed that Demetrius should take to wife Ptolemais, the daughter of Ptolemy.[4]

Here we see a whirlwind of Successor diplomacy, with both Seleucus and Ptolemy in favour of *rapprochement* with Demetrius, who then successfully reclaimed Cilicia. The big loser was Pleistarchus, ousted from Cilicia, and by default Cassander. Demetrius also had a reunion with his third wife, only to lose her shortly after, and finally the prospect of another marriage (he and Ptolemais were to marry much later). In the longer run, Demetrius would have a falling-out with Seleucus over Cilicia as the latter was keen to take control of it himself. But for now, Demetrius' attention turned back to Greece.

The King of Macedon

By the mid 290s BC Athens had slid back into demagoguery under the tyrant Lachares. Earlier backed by Cassander, he'd used mercenaries to seize power and then stripped the city temples of their wealth to pay them. This included the gold from the cult statue of Athena in the Parthenon. When the great and the good of the city reached out to Demetrius for help, he saw his opportunity. He was soon blockading the city, finally securing it in 294 BC after Lachares fled to Beoetia. Demetrius then pardoned the inhabitants for turning their backs on him after Ipsus and installed a new system of government which was anything but democratic. Gone were the glory days of Antigonid ascendancy when, as a young man, he'd bathed in the adulation of a grateful city. Now he needed stability, and abolished the cyclical rotation of the secretaries of the Athenian council and the election of the archon high magistrates by allotment. In effect, he had restored oligarchical government of exactly the kind he'd removed back in 307 BC.

However, these dramatic events in Athens did not take place in isolation. In the north, equal drama had also engulfed Macedon. There Cassander had died of a cerebral oedema in Pella in 297 BC, and though his two sons Alexander V and Antipater I succeeded him, they both proved weak kings. They soon fell out, with the younger then calling on Demetrius for assistance. This set him against the Epirot king Pyrrhus, now back on his throne and without familial ties with Demetrius given the death of Deidameia. For Pyrrhus, Macedon was within his own sphere of influence. Soon he had seized Ambracia on the western borders of Macedon. In response, an emboldened Demetrius now invaded Macedonia, quickly killing his initial sponsor, Alexander, and seizing control of the kingdom himself by 294 BC. This was an astonishing recovery for a man who, only seven years earlier, had seen the Antigonid dream all but wiped out at Ipsus. Here Lysimachus then helped secure him in power as when Antipater fled to Thrace the successor had him murdered, wiping out the Antipatrid line.

Was Demetrius satisfied with the Macedonian throne alone? Probably not. Remember he had grown up in the finery of his father's Asian court in Celaenae. He loved the trappings of power, both good and bad. Further, only seven years earlier he and his father were ruling much of Alexander the Great's vast empire. This was a man of huge ambition. In that context, it seems likely he was only interested in using Macedon as a power base to rebuild his strength. He knew it was highly likely conflict would soon be renewed with the surviving Diadochi. That would give him one last chance to become the true heir to Alexander.

Sadly for Demetrius, the Macedonian aristocracy reciprocated his lack of warmth and empathy. Plutarch portrays a stark picture of two cultures clashing, saying:

> And not only by such displays did he vex his subjects, who were unused to them, but his luxurious ways of living were also offensive, and above all else the difficulty of getting access to him or conversing with him [essential to rule successfully in the Macedonian heartland]. For either he would give no audience at all, or he was stern and harsh with his auditors. For instance, he kept an embassy from the Athenians, for whose favour he was more solicitous than for that of any other Greeks, two years in waiting; and when a single envoy came to him from Sparta, he thought himself despised, and was incensed. However, when he cried, 'What meanest thou? Have the Spartans sent but one

envoy?' he got the neat and laconic reply, 'Yea, O king, to one man.' On one occasion, when he was thought to be riding abroad in a more affable mood than usual, and seemed to encounter his subjects without displeasure, there was a large concourse of people who presented him with written petitions. He received them all and folded them away in his cloak, whereupon the people were delighted and escorted him on his way; but when he came to the bridge over the Axius, he shook out the folds of his cloak and cast all the petitions into the river. This was a great vexation to the Macedonians, who thought themselves insulted, not ruled, and they called to mind, or listened to those who called to mind, how reasonable Philip II used to be in such matters, and how accessible. An old woman once assailed Demetrius as he was passing by, and demanded many times that he give her a hearing. 'I have no time,' said Demetrius. 'Then don't be king,' screamed the old woman. Demetrius was stung to the quick, and after thinking upon the matter, went back to his house, and postponing everything else, for several days devoted himself entirely to those who wished audience of him, beginning with the old woman who had rebuked him.[5]

Such rapprochement proved short lived, with things not improved by two failed campaigns against Pyrrhus to the west and the Aetolians to the north. Then, while Demetrius was distracted fighting there, the ageing Lysimachus invaded his outlying territories to the east, with the support of Seleucus and Ptolemy, who once more sensed an opportunity. Soon Lysimachus had recovered any of his territories in western Anatolia previously lost to the Antigonids, while Seleucus took most of Cilicia and Ptolemy recovered Cyprus, eastern Cilicia and Lycia.

At this turn of events, Demetrius' support in Pella quickly evaporated, his rapid demise there aided by diplomatic and financial interventions by Lysimachus and Pyrrhus. In 288 BC he was forced to flee as rebellion broke out, with control of the kingdom divided between Lysimachus and Pyrrhus. Phila did not join him, either dying of natural causes or by suicide. Demetrius re-emerged in Greece where he remained popular and, by appointing his son Antigonus Gonatus to control Antigonid interests there, hoped to rebuild his position again. However, once more Athens again turned its back on him, though he kept control of its harbour Piraeus, where he'd leapt ashore to such great fanfare so long ago. That meant he still had his fleet.

Anabasis

Demetrius had now fallen from the lofty heights of power twice. Yet he still believed he had a chance to recover the Antigonid position again. Whether through pure self-belief or narcissism is difficult to define. However, he now had his final throw of the dice, aiming to emulate his hero Alexander in a drive eastwards on a huge *anabasis*.

He was still hugely popular with the various military factions across Greece, including his own remaining troops and still-impressive fleet. First, he signed a peace deal with Pyrrhus to protect his rear. His initial target would be Lysimachus in Anatolia, before he turned his attention to Seleucid Syria. Romm makes the case that, for military leaders in the Classical world, military life could become an addiction.[6] That was certainly the case with Alexander, and here with Demetrius too. He simply didn't know when to stop. Neither did Pyrrhus, who reneged on his agreement with Demetrius as soon as the latter headed for Asia.

Demetrius ignored this entirely. For him, there was one goal. To emulate Alexander. If he could do that, he thought, all his previous reverses would be forgotten. To be fair, so did the thousands of troops who signed up for his expedition. Soon he landed in western Anatolia, where in many areas he was welcomed. He received a particularly friendly reception in Miletus, where he finally married Ptolemais, most likely with Ptolemy's approval, such was the fast-moving pace of Diadochi politics. She became the mother of one of his children,

Demetrius the Fair. The bride was given away at the wedding by Eurydice, sister of his first wife Phila and mother of his new wife. Demetrius then took Sardis, where some of Lysimachus' generals defected to the Antigonid cause. However, sadly for Demetrius, that proved the high point of his *anabasis*. Plutarch provides the detail as things turned against him once more, saying:

> When Agathocles, the son of Lysimachus, came against him with an army, Demetrius retired into Phrygia [and no doubt Celaenae]; he had determined, if once he could reach Armenia, to bring Media to revolt and attempt to reach the upper provinces, which afforded an ejected commander many refuges and retreats. Agathocles followed him, and though Demetrius had the advantage in their engagements, he was shut off from getting provisions and forage, and was in great straits; besides, his soldiers were suspicious that he was trying to make his way towards Armenia and Media.[7]

It seems that here Demetrius had been strategically outmanoeuvred. Trapped in the central Anatolian plateau, he could get neither forage, nor receive shipments from home.[8] Soon pack animals and unfamiliar fruit and vegetables were being eaten, with many of his troops falling ill. The rest began to starve. In desperate straits, and with a third fall from grace looming, he forced a crossing of the fast-flowing Lycus river in an attempt to push east. This proved ill-advised, with many of his men drowning in the strong current.

Still he pushed on, most likely for lack of choice. Desperate to find his men food, he crossed the Taurus Mountains and passed through the Cilician Gates which led to the fertile plains of northern Syria. Agathocles remained close behind. For him his job was now done: he had driven the bedraggled Demetrius and the remnants of his army out of his father's territory into that of Seleucus. He locked the Cilician Gates. There would be no going back for Demetrius that way.

Once in northwestern Syria Demetrius struggled to control his starving men. Soon they were ravaging the plentiful surrounding countryside. Knowing the damage this would do to his relationship with Seleucus (his son-in-law remember), he wrote to him to request clemency, an odd thing to do considering that, if his *anabasis* was to succeed, he would need to conquer at least some Seleucid territory. However, when Seleucus read the letter he was moved to sympathy, and set about planning to help his fellow Successor. However, a courtier called Patrocles then intervened, reminding the Seleucid court how dangerous Demetrius was. He won the day, and an army was gathered.

Demetrius was clearly expecting succour from Seleucus, and despaired when he saw him approach with his troops. Knowing things were all nearly over, he asked for a small kingdom in the Taurus Mountains so that he could be the king of at least something. Seleucus refused, but knowing winter was on the way, he allowed Demetrius and his troops to remain in a place called Cataonia for two months. To make sure the besieger behaved, he then closed all the regional passes.

Demetrius remained there for longer than two months, but he and his men had to endure a brutal winter. Eventually he was forsaken by his troops who had had enough, and in 286 BC was forced to surrender to Seleucus. This put the latter in a very difficult position given his fellow Diadochi, particularly Lysimachus, would love to have seen the last Antigonid removed permanently. To Seleucus' credit he didn't execute him, but kept him in gilded imprisonment somewhere near Antioch-on-the-Orontes. There, despite Demetrius' son, Antigonus Gonatus, offering his own person and possessions to free him, he remained for the rest of his life. Demetrius died three years later, of disease, alcoholism or gluttony, or a combination of all three. Seleucus had him cremated with due honours and sent him back to his son in Greece in a gilded urn. There he was given a fine funeral in Corinth. So ended the Antigonid royal line, not with a bang but with the mildest of whimpers, a sad end for the ultimate man who would be king.

Conclusion

What to make of Demetrius? The brilliant-but-flawed Successor who lit up his own world, and later that of the Romans too, but a man who ultimately succumbed to the treachery of the post-Alexandrian power politics that had already cost the life of his father. A man who was king twice, and nearly a third time. Yet one who fell from grace each time. Once could be construed as unlucky, and maybe twice, but not three times.

Given that his life ended in captivity, it would be very easy to call Demetrius a failure. At one stage he and his father were set to recreate the empire of Alexander, leading the most powerful military establishment of their Hellenistic world. However, though he clearly knew how to fight a war, often succeeding against great odds, administration wasn't Demetrius' thing. That is what ultimately cost him the Macedonian throne. That, and the debauchery, all very un-Macedonian when played out in public. He was clearly very driven and resilient, with enormous self-confidence, but with an inability to take wise counsel when needed. Perhaps that was his most fatal weakness.

On a personal level I am also struck by how desperate the older Demetrius was to redeem himself from what he would surely have viewed as the low point of his life. This was leaving his father fatally exposed at Ipsus, and then being unable to save the old man. Surely, his deathbed wish was the hope that the father he loved so much would forgive him in an afterlife he certainly believed in. But what of his longer-term legacy? In true Antigonid fashion, it was mixed.

The Hellenistic World After Demetrius

Back in Greece, with Demetrius now gone, Lysimachus and Pyrrhus launched a campaign to the south, driving Antigonus Gonatas out of Thessaly and eventually out of Athens. However, they fell out over who should have the spoils of final victory. Lysimachus then turned on Pyrrhus and drove him out of Macedon, taking control of the entire kingdom.

However, dynastic struggles in Egypt now intervened. The elderly Ptolemy had made his younger son, Ptolemy Philadelphus, his heir rather than his elder son, Ptolemy Ceraunus (an appropriate epithet, meaning thunderbolt). The latter promptly fled to join Seleucus in the east who was then dragged into the succession squabbles of the Ptolemies after Ptolemy himself died peacefully in 282 BC. This soon set him against Lysimachus, the two meeting in battle at Corupedium in Lydia in 281 BC, with Seleucus emerging the victor and Lysimachus dead. This proved the last battle between Alexander's successors, and although victory gave Seleucus nominal control over most of Alexander's empire except Egypt, his ascendancy was short lived. This was because when he crossed the Hellespont to take possession of Lysimachus' European territories in Thrace and Macedonia, he was promptly assassinated by Ptolemy Ceraunus, who then seized the Macedonian throne, an extreme example of Hellenistic *realpolitik*. However, the latter's success was equally short lived as, after defeating an initial challenge from Antigonus Gonatus, he himself fell in battle against the most unexpected of enemies, the invading Galatians.

The Galatians were the eastern Gauls who had migrated through the Balkans from the 280s BC and eventually founded the Galatian kingdoms in central Anatolia. Their arrival on the borders of Macedon coincided with similar Gallic migrations in the west. They proved to be fearsome warriors with a military system featuring a chariot-riding aristocracy (later replaced with cavalry) and line-of-battle infantry armed with short spears and long, slashing swords, who were renowned for their fearsome charge. After the demise of Ptolemy Ceraunus, they were eventually driven out of the Balkans by the Macedonians and the Greek *poleis*, hence their arrival in Anatolia.

Back in Macedon, a short period of instability followed the Galatians' passage through the region, with Antigonus Gonatus finally emerging as the new king in 277 BC. He proved a capable monarch, being a far better administrator than his father. It was he who provided the stability that allowed the kingdom to recover from decades of strife during the Successor wars and, most recently, the Galatian invasions. It was also he who established the longest-lasting iteration of the Antigonid dynasty, set to continue until the kingdom's final, catastrophic defeat by Rome.

To this point, the Hellenistic kingdoms established after the collapse of Alexander's empire had dominated their known world. However, the rise to dominance in Italy of Rome now fundamentally changed that dynamic. Founded on the eastern banks of the River Tiber in the early first millennium BC, this small town had grown rapidly, and through grit and determination came first to dominate its own Latium locale, then Etruria to the north, next much of Magna Graecia to the south, and finally found itself coming into regular contact with the Hellenistic world. The first time was, appropriately, through conflict when the restless Pyrrhus invaded Italy in late 281 BC.

Rome's growing engagement with the Hellenistic world was most evident in its four wars against the kingdom of Macedon in the late third and early-to-mid-second centuries BC. The first occurred in the context of Rome's Second Punic War against Hannibal's Carthaginian Empire when, at the height of the latter's success in Italy, the ambitious Macedonian king, Philip V (a direct descendant of Demetrius), set out to interfere with Rome's client states in Illyria. He was then caught out rashly trying to agree a treaty with Hannibal when the latter was still in Italy.

Soon the First Macedonian War began, which lasted from 214 to 205 BC. Here, Rome's first intervention in the Balkans against Macedonian interests was half-hearted, understandable given its focus on defending its Italian home territories from Hannibal, and eventually the Peace of Phoenice ended the conflict on terms favourable to the Macedonians.

Emboldened, Philip now began to harass some of the Greek *poleis* in the Aegean and Anatolia who were allies of Rome. This was a direct challenge to Roman interests and the Second Macedonian War broke out in 200 BC. At the outset, the Romans landed in force in the eastern Balkans, fighting a minor campaign there in 199 BC before invading Thessaly in 198 BC. The major engagement of the war then took place at Cynoscephalae in 197 BC, with the first crushing defeat of a Hellenistic army at the hands of the legions of Rome.

Philip's defeat at Cynosophelae ended the war, the Macedonian king realizing he now had no chance of ultimate victory. He agreed peace with the Romans on the most onerous of terms, including the loss of most of his navy, the payment of a huge indemnity and the permanent loss of any Macedonian territories abroad.

An uneasy peace now settled on the Balkans. However, when Philip died in 179 BC, he was succeeded by his son Perseus, an ambitious young man who quickly moved to restore Macedon's international influence. Sadly for the new king, his aggressive actions against the neighbouring Greek *poleis* in Thessaly soon drew the attention of Rome again, and when Perseus was implicated in a plot to assassinate a Roman ally, the Senate declared war. This began the Third Macedonian War. Here, though Perseus was initially successful, on 22 June 168 BC the Macedonian phalanx and Roman legions (this time under the command of Lucius Aemilius Paullus) met once more at the Battle of Pydna. In this engagement the flexibility of the Roman legionary maniples proved the decisive factor after the phalanx was drawn onto rough ground, and soon another massacre occurred, with the Macedonians crushed once more.

After the end of the conflict, the Romans decided to end Macedonian resistance once and for all, with Perseus taken back to Rome in chains, where he either died in captivity or received clemency, depending on the source you follow. So ended the Antigonid dynasty. Much more importantly, the Romans decided to break up the Kingdom of Macedon permanently into four nominally independent republics, all of which were required to pay tribute to Rome. The Romans clearly expected this arrangement to stabilize northern Greece but, instead, it produced a state of chronic disorder. Then, in 152 BC, a pretender to the Macedonian throne called Andriscus emerged, claiming without evidence to be a son of Perseus. His misguided attempts to re-establish the Macedonian monarchy under the guidance of ambitious nobles there provoked the Fourth Macedonian War, this only lasting a year when in 148 BC the Romans under Quintus Caecilius Metellus crushed the rebellion with ease. The entire geographic area of the former Kingdom of Macedon was then finally made into a Roman province. By that time Seleucid power had also been broken by Rome, since Antiochus III (the Great) had been badly defeated at the Battle of Magnesia in 190 BC.

The final conflict between the mainland Greeks and Romans was the Achaean War, an uprising led by the Achaean League, the long-standing alliance featuring the Achaean and other Peloponnesian *poleis*. The war broke out in 146 BC in the aftermath of the Fourth Macedonian War. Frustrated by repeated demands to commit its legions to deal with such insurgencies in Greece, and the internal squabbles of the *poleis*, the Romans decided to deal with the Achaeans and their allies harshly, sending the Consul Lucius Mummius there with an army of 27,000 men. This quickly destroyed the Achaean army at the Battle of Corinth, where a force of 14,000 infantry and 600 cavalry was destroyed in detail.

After his victory, Mummius entered Corinth under arms, putting all of the men there to the sword before selling the women and children into slavery. Then, in a pattern set to be repeated time and again over the next century, all of the city's statues, paintings and works of art were seized for shipment to Rome. The once mighty city was then razed to the ground, in the same manner as Carthage in the same year at the close of the Third Punic War. Mummius' behaviour here is perhaps anachronistic, given he was generally thought a moderate. However, clearly here he was acting on the instructions from the Senate to make an example of Corinth, with a view to ensuring there was no further trouble in Greece. On his return to Rome, he celebrated a triumph and gained the title Achaicus, using the wealth derived from his Greek campaign to erect a theatre in his name that was noted for its improved acoustics and seating, features modelled on examples he had seen in Greece.

The Achaean War marked the effective end of Greek political independence, with the Romans eventually deciding to annex much of mainland Greece. This initially became part of the Roman province of Macedonia, though some cities including Athens and Sparta retained a degree of self-rule. In the first century BC, a final attempt to remove Roman influence there in the context of the Mithridatic Wars dramatically failed. After this, Macedonia and Greece became a key battleground in the later civil wars of the Roman Republic. When the latter concluded, with Octavian the last man standing (later becoming Augustus, the first emperor), the entirety of the Balkans peninsula was over time finally incorporated into the world of Rome as the provinces of Macedonia, Epirus and Achaea.

The end of the Achaean War also saw the rest of the Hellenistic world in sad decline. The only significant remaining power in the Aegean was pro-Roman Pergamon, whose last king, Attalus III, bequeathed his kingdom to Rome in his will when he died in 133 BC. Meanwhile the Seleucid Empire was slowly collapsing under pressure from Roman interests in the west and Parthian aggression in the east, while Ptolemaic Egypt was finally subsumed into the world of Rome as the province of Aegyptus after the dramatic death of Cleopatra VII

Philopater in 30 BC. Thus ended the world of Antigonus and Demetrius, subsumed into the ever-expanding sphere of Roman power which now held sway on three continents. Even Alexander would have been impressed.

Appendix A

Pen Portraits of the Diadochi

The Wars of the Successors, which erupted after Alexander's death in Babylon in 323 BC, featured a cast of thousands fit to grace anything in modern popular fiction. Here, to act as a resource for the reader, I give pen portraits of the leading Diadochi who played such a key role in the stories of Antigonus Monophthalmus and Demetrius (both covered in detail in the book rather than here).

Antipater

Antipater was the elder statesman entrusted with the regency in Macedon while Alexander led his *anabasis* eastwards. Born around 397 BC, little is known of him before 342 BC when he was first appointed regent by Philip II (Alexander's father) while that king campaigned in Thrace and Scythia to the north and west. Then, as later, he was a loyal and active *strategos* for the Argeads, sending Macedonian troops to Euboea later that year to suppress Athenian interference in the *poleis* there. The trust placed in Antipater by the Argeads is next shown when he was sent by Phillip to Athens after Chaeronea to become the king's ambassador for two years, his task to negotiate a peace treaty with a city that still viewed its northern conqueror as brutish and uncouth. Showing the wisdom of experience, Antipater won over local support by arriving with the bones of those who had fallen in the battle.

Next, when Philip was assassinated, Antipater acted as the key steadying force in the kingdom, aiding Alexander in his succession struggle. He had long championed the boy and, when the new king headed to Thrace on his Danubian campaign in 335 BC, Antipater was appointed regent a second time. Shortly afterwards, Antipater joined Parmenion in advising the young king against setting out on his *anabasis* until he had secured the Argead succession by marrying a Macedonian bride of noble lineage and having a son. This was sound advice given what was to follow. While such guidance was ignored, Antipater was still held in high enough regard to be appointed regent a third time in 334 BC when Alexander's great campaign began. Further, in addition to running the king's government in Pella, Antipater was also made *strategos* of Europe, an additional position he still held when Alexander died.

Cassander

Of the early life of Cassander, Antipater's son, little is known other than Aristotle taught him alongside Alexander and the other companions. He first rises to prominence when representing his father in Babylon in 323 BC, where Alexander treated him with open hostility, allegedly smashing his head into a wall after Cassander laughed at the eastern ways of the court. Pausanius says Alexander's animosity for Antipater's son was reciprocated, explaining that:

> Cassander was mainly influenced by hatred of Alexander. He destroyed the whole house of Alexander to the bitter end.[1]

After Alexander's death, Cassander was appointed senior cavalry commander of the 'home army', a position he still held at the time of his father's death. The primary sources portray him as impetuous and ambitious. Athenaeus adds that Antipater's son had to sit upright at banquets when a grown man as he had failed to spear a wild boar as a youth and so was banned from reclining at table.[2] Whether or not such a negative reputation was deserved, Cassander is often viewed today as a Herod-like figure, forever damned for wiping out Alexander's line.

Polyperchon

Polyperchon was born in western Macedon at Tymphaea near the Epirot border. He served with Alexander for most of the *anabasis* in the east, initially as a bodyguard and then being given command of the Tymphaean regiment of the phalanx after Issus. Polyperchon held this post until 324 BC when he returned to Macedon with Craterus' veterans. He then served as deputy to Antipater's son Cassander during the Lamian War against Athens and the Aetolian League, after which he held the post of governor in Pella. His reputation was one of steadfast loyalty, not intellect.

Perdiccas

Perdiccas was the clear winner in the first stage of the post-Alexandrian world. The son of a nobleman called Orontes from the leading Macedonian house of Orestis (a mountainous tribal district in upper Macedonia), he was of similar age to Alexander. As a young man he was given command of his native battalion in the phalanx and accompanied Alexander in his campaigns in Illyria in 335 BC, and then a year later in Greece when he was severely injured during the siege of Thebes. However, he quickly recovered and then accompanied the king throughout his campaigns in the east, becoming one of the seven bodyguards in 330 BC. His seniority is shown by the fact that when Alexander ordered his leading generals to marry Persian wives at Susa in 324 BC, only four Macedonians married actual princesses, these being the king himself, his favourite Hephaestion, Craterus and Perdiccas. Well thought of as a military leader, Perdiccas then replaced

Hephaestion as *chiliarch* of the first regiment of the Companions when the latter died. This role also included being the king's vizier, his highest-ranking political advisor. Thus he was best placed among the future Successors to become regent when Alexander died.

Ptolemy

Ptolemy was to become one of the great figures of the Hellenistic world, and founder of the Ptolemaic dynasty in Egypt, where he died as Ptolemy I Soter (Saviour) in 282 BC. Born around 367 BC, much is known about his life both before Alexander's death and as a Successor, given he was a prolific historian in his own right and founder of the great library in Alexandria, where he spent much of his later life preserving Alexander's memory. The son of a noble called Lagus, though rumoured to be a bastard son of Phillip II, he was eleven years older than Alexander, to whom he became a childhood friend and later a trusted confidant. Ptolemy served with the king from his first campaigns, and then played a key role in the later *anabasis* in the east. At the Battle of Issus in 333 BC, he commanded troops on the left flank under Parmenion, along with Craterus, and later accompanied Alexander on his journey to the oracle at the Siwa oasis. During the Persian campaign he also became one of the king's bodyguards and his personal food taster. Ptolemy's first independent command was in the upper satrapies during the campaign against Bessus, whom he captured and handed over to Alexander for execution.[3] Later, during Alexander's campaign in India, Ptolemy commanded the advanced guard at the Siege of Aornos, and then fought at the Battle of the Hydaspes River.

Lysimachus

Lysimachus was born in 361 BC into a high-ranking noble family in Pella, later being the founder of the short-lived Thraco-Macedonian dynasty in Thrace. He was the second son of Agathocles, a close friend of Philip II who shared control of the king's council and was an Argead court favourite. Lysimachus was appointed a royal bodyguard to Philip prior to Alexander's accession, and to the latter in 328 BC. He played a leading military role in Alexander's eastern campaigns, particularly in India. He led a maritime operation aboard a 30-oared vessel during the Hydaspes battle, later sailing down the Indus to the Indian Ocean.

Eumenes

Eumenes was Greek by birth and a native of Cardia in the Thracian Chersonese who, at an early age, was employed as Philip II's private secretary, a role he continued under Alexander. A royal favourite, he was given military command in the last year of Alexander's life with responsibility for a *hipparchia* of Companion cavalry. However, despite his undeniable skills as an administrator and soldier, he never enjoyed the full support of the Macedonians at court, given his ethnicity and royal familiarity as secretary. Later as a Successor, this developed into outright hostility to him by many of his contemporaries.

Craterus

Craterus was the son of a Macedonian nobleman called Alexander of Orestis, and the brother of Amphoterus. The latter was the maritime *strategos* who helped subdue the eastern Mediterranean for Alexander in 333 BC. Craterus is first recorded in high office commanding the phalanx and other infantry on the left wing at Issus in 333 BC. Later, after the removal of Philotas and Parmenion, he was trusted with independent commands by Alexander, the first being in Hyrcania (southeast of the Caspian Sea in modern Iran) on a mission against the Tapurians. Later, at the Hydaspes, he commanded Alexander's reserve, joining the battle during the final pursuit phase. His favour with Alexander is shown by the fact that, like his fellow Orestian Perdiccas, he was one of the four Macedonians allowed to marry a princess (Amastris, daughter of Darius III's brother Oxyathres) at Susa in 324 BC. He was also the one trusted with leading back the veterans to Macedon the same year, with Alexander set to have him replace Antipater as regent in Pella.

Seleucus

Seleucus, like Ptolemy, was destined to emerge from the Successor wars as a giant of the age. Born around 358 BC in Europos in northern Macedonia, he was the son of one of Philip II's generals called Antiochus. Also one of Alexander's *syntrophus* and later a *paides* (page), he fought throughout the eastern campaigns with the king (including in Anatolia, Persia, Bactria, Sogdiana and India), rising in 327 BC to become the commander of the Argyraspides (Silver Shields) (as the Hypaspists were by then known) and later being promoted to the royal bodyguard. He remained close to the king and was one of the friends who attended the temple of Serapis the night before Alexander died.

Appendix B

Alexander the Great's Battles

Given their importance as references when narrating the wider story of Demetrius, here I detail Alexander the Great's four main set piece battles at Granicus River, Ipsus, Gaugamela and Hydaspes River.

The Battle of the Granicus River

Persian military activity operated on two levels, royal and satrapal. In the first instance, usually in wars of conquest or to tackle existential threats, an army was gathered from across the wider empire and led by the king in person. In the latter case, the army was more regional in nature, led by one or more of the king's satraps (provincial governors). In 334 BC, as Alexander crossed into Asia, Darius' initial response was to rely on his local satraps in Anatolia to deal with the upstart Macedonian king. Only if they failed, which he thought highly unlikely, would he then become directly involved with the full royal army.

Here, having been caught out by Parmenion's earlier Macedonian expedition, Darius now moved with unusual speed. Using the empire's sophisticated system of royal trunk roads, the king's royal couriers swiftly delivered his orders to the satraps ranged across Anatolia. By early May, these and their military commanders had gathered to consider their campaigning strategy at Zeleia, the Homeric town in the Troad at the foot of Mount Ila. Darius placed the local regional governor, Arsites, in charge of the gathering, and also the subsequent campaign, he being the long-standing satrap of Hellespontine Phrygia. This region covered the northwestern coast of Anatolia where Parmenion's expedition had earlier campaigned, and where many of the latter's troops still remained. Arsites was already known to Alexander as the satrap who had been the first Persian leader to send aid to Perinthus when Philip II had besieged the city in 340 BC.

Arsites was joined at Zeleia by the leading nobles from the Persian west, all keen to show their metal against Alexander and impress Darius. Foremost were two more key satraps, Arsames of Cilicia and Spithridates of Lydia and Ionia. The latter had a particular interest in stopping the Macedonian advance at the earliest opportunity, given that his satrapy was the location of many of the leading Ionian Greek cities that Alexander was hoping to liberate. These included Ephesus, Miletus and Priene. This key satrapy also included Sardis, Darius' regional capital where the king had an imperial palace and treasury. Meanwhile, other key noblemen arriving at Zeleia included Spithridates' brother Rhoesaces, Darius' son-in-law Mithridates, Rheomithres (whose son Phrasaortes was later appointed satrap of Persis by Alexander), and the cavalry commanders Petenes and Niphates.

However, the key figure attending the gathering at Zeleia was Memnon of Rhodes, the mercenary Greek *strategos* who had earlier defeated Parmenion and his expeditionary force near Magnesia. We know far more about him than any of the other leaders at Zeleia, not surprising given all of our primary sources are Greek. Born around 380 BC, he had served the Persian Empire for most of his life, alongside his brother Mentor. Indeed, their sister had married the Phrygian satrap Artabazos II. Memnon knew the Macedonians well, having accompanied Artabazos into exile in Philip II's court at Pella after the satrap's failed rebellion against Artaxerxes III in 352 BC (the two taking their eleven sons and daughters with them). However, Mentor had stayed loyal to the then Persian king, later distinguishing himself in Persian service fighting the last native Egyptian pharaoh, Nectanebo II, the Greek playing a key leadership role in the decisive Battle of Pelusium in 343 BC.

Eventually, Mentor persuaded Memnon to return to Persian service after four years in Macedon. Mentor died in 340 BC, after which Memnon married his brother's wife Barsine (a daughter of Artabazos), she later becoming the lover of Alexander the Great and mother of Hercules, the Macedonian king's supposed illegitimate son.

In 339 BC, Memnon helped the city of Byzantium defend itself against Philip's siege, and subsequently led the Persian campaign against Parmenion's expeditionary force. Then, when the Macedonian king was assassinated, Memnon urged Darius to foment a rebellion against Macedonian hegemony in Greece, knowing the difficulty Alexander faced in securing his hold on the throne. Now, as the Persians gathered at Zeleia to tackle the new king's invasion, Memnon became one of the leading commanders of the combined satrapal army.

The speedy response of Darius to Alexander's invasion wrong-footed the young king who quickly changed his invasion strategy. Instead of heading southwards along the western coastline of Anatolia, where he had planned to quickly liberate the Greek cities one by one, he now headed northwest along the coast of the Hellespont and Phrygia to meet the Persian challenge. To ensure a speedy advance, he left much of his invasion force behind, taking just 18,000 troops overall. This included most of the cavalry including the Companions and *prodromoi*, all of the Hypaspists and available phalanx, and his Agrianian javelinmen and archers, the latter including the highly experienced Cretans. At this point Memnon advised a scorched earth policy to buy time for a royal army to be gathered under Darius, which he felt would guarantee victory.

However, the Persians were reluctant to further damage the regional economy given the severe disruption caused by Parmenion's earlier campaign. They therefore decided to challenge Alexander directly instead. Having been forewarned by Memnon, and then fought

Parmenion, the Persians were keenly aware of the Macedonian pike phalanx's fearsome reputation. Therefore, they moved their army away from the open plains around Zeleia where the terrain was more suitable for Alexander's army. Heading westward, the Persians soon found themselves among the hills and streams on Mount Ida's western slopes. There they built a large camp on the eastern side of the Granicus River. They then prepared to defend the waterway against any attempt by Alexander to cross. This river gently meanders northeast to the Sea of Marmara through the plains of Phrygia, and while not a significant waterway at that time of year (at its deepest it was only 1 metre) it still presented a formidable obstacle to the Macedonians.

Arrayed against them on the eastern bank, the Persians deployed in an unusual formation given their plan was to defend the steep-sided riverbank. Most contemporary sources suggest that instead of positioning their heavy infantry atop the steep riverbank, as one would expect, they instead deployed the entirety of their cavalry across the front of their battleline, with the hoplite foot soldiers relegated to a position atop a hill to the rear. Many have speculated one reason for this might be the Persians being wary of the Greek mercenaries' loyalty, especially when fighting compatriots (this certainly the case with Alexander's Greek allied cavalry). However, another reason was the desire of the various foremost Persian noblemen leading their regional retinues to achicvc glory on thc battlcficld. Ccrtainly, thcir disposition indicatcs this, as all played a prominent role in the ensuing battle, leading from the front and with many seeking to confront Alexander in person. In that regard, facing Alexander on the Persian left were Memnon with his sons and Arsames, each with their own cavalry contingent. Next, moving left to right, were Arsites with his Paphlagonian horsemen and Spithridates with his elite Hyrcanian guard cavalry who together commanded the Persian centre. Finally, on the right wing, Rheomithres led a large contingent of Median and Bactrian horse.

As Alexander looked across the Granicus it quickly became clear the Persians were refusing to advance. Diodorus Siculus describes the scene, saying:

> The Persians, resting on high ground, made no move, intending to fall upon their foe as he crossed the river, for they supposed they could easily carry the day when the Macedonian phalanx was divided [the last a reference to the expected disruption as it crossed the river].[1]

By now it was late afternoon and Alexander decided to take the offensive. First, he ordered the *prodromoi*, Paeonian light horse, their supporting Companions and a unit of Hypaspists to force the river under Amyntas, targeting the extreme left of the Persian line. By this time, having ridden up and down the Macedonian line making final dispositions, Alexander had arrived back to take his position on the extreme right wing with the remaining Companions, alongside Philotas. Positioned at the apex of the wedge of his own 300-strong Royal Squadron (*ile basilike*) of the Companions, he now gave the command for a general advance, the primary sources saying he plunged into the water first. Meanwhile, his spearhead of lighter horse, targeting Memnon and Arsames, had already waded through the river and reached the far bank where they were targeted by the javelins and bows of the Persian horse. Many unarmoured *prodromoi* and Paeonians were cut down, and the Macedonian advance quickly wavered. Sensing an easy victory, the Persians on the left wing now surged forward down the muddy bank, including Memnon himself, with more and more drawn into the engagement from the centre.

Soon, with weight of numbers increasingly in their favour, the Persians began to push the Macedonians back over the river, leaving twenty-five Companions dead on the eastern riverbank. However, urgent help was on the way. Alexander now unveiled a tactical masterstroke from the extreme right flank. Having led the majority of the Companions into the Granicus, they now passed behind the initial spearhead, crossing right to left where they then charged at full speed up the eastern riverbank into Memnon and Arsames' surging Persian left-wing cavalry. This positioned them at the juncture of the Persian left and centre.

A desperate melee ensued, with the Macedonians having the advantage of their long *xyston* lances. Soon the Persian cavalry in the river and atop the bank broke, with the Companions then forcing the eastern shore of the Granicus to pursue into the flank of the Persian centre. The primary sources now focus entirely on Alexander as he led his companions from the front. Arrian says the king deliberately made himself as conspicuous as possible through the 'brightness of his arms' and the brilliant white plume atop his helmet.[2] This certainly attracted the attention of the Persians, many of whom now sought to engage Alexander directly. This included Mithridates who was in Arsites' command in the Persian centre. Darius' son-in-law headed directly for Alexander who, seeing the danger, counter-charged with his close guard. A desperate fight ensued, with the Macedonian king shattering his own *xyston* and borrowing another from Demaratas of Corinth, a Greek Companion recruited by Philip. With this he impaled Mithridates in the face, killing him instantly. However, there was no respite for the Macedonian king, with another Persian nobleman charging into the melee. This was Mithradates' brother Rhoesaces who aimed a blow at Alexander's head, the king dodging the savage strike just in time, with the Persian's sword slicing off part of his plume and cracking his helmet. Alexander ran him through with the same *xyston*. By this time Spithridates had closed on the king with his Hyrcanian guard, the Lydian satrap aiming another blow at Alexander's head. However, Cleitus the Black, Alexander's close bodyguard in the battle, attacked the Persian first and severed his arm, saving Alexander's life.

By this time Alexander's centre and left had begun to surge across the eastern bank of the Granicus. Seeing this, especially after the loss of so many leaders in the savage cavalry fight, the Persians began to fall back. Then, when Parmenion charged the Persian right wing with his Thessalians and Thracians, the Persian cavalry broke and began to flee the battlefield, along with any of the surviving Persian leaders. This left just the Greek hoplite mercenaries on the hill at the rear, no doubt bemused at the sudden change in Persian fortunes.

Alexander now rallied his troops to prevent a headlong pursuit of the Persian cavalry. He then turned his attention to the Greek heavy foot soldiers. Their leaders first tried to negotiate a truce with Alexander and, when this was turned down, begged for mercy. However, the Macedonian king was infuriated by what he saw as their treachery in fighting with the Persians and ordered a general attack. First Parmenion with the Thessalians and Thracians circled to the left of the Greek line. Then Alexander with the Companions positioned himself on the right. Finally, the phalanx drew up to pin the Greeks in place to their front. When all was in place, the Macedonian king ordered a general assault, and a terrible slaughter began. Though the Greeks fought desperately, with nothing to lose, the engagement was short and one-sided. Plutarch has Alexander leading the way and charging headlong into the fray, with his charger (not Bucephalus) killed from under him when a *doru* (spear) was driven into the horse's ribs.[3] However, the end was never in doubt and soon 18,000 hoplites were slain, with the surviving 2,000 sent back to Macedon in chains where a short future working as slaves in the mines awaited. As to other casualties, if one takes the primary sources at face value, 2,500 Persian cavalry were slain, while the Macedonians lost 85 cavalry and 30 infantry, most when fighting the doomed Greek foot soldiers. Though the latter figures for Alexander's losses are improbable, they do show the scale of his victory. Meanwhile, of the surviving Persian leaders, Arsites made good his escape but later committed suicide, while Memnon chose not to fall with his Greek compatriots but also fled. Shortly afterwards, Darius made him the governor of all of the western satrapies, he later leading the failed defence of Halicarnassus and finally being killed during the siege of Mytilene.

The Battle of Issus

Many view the later battle of Gaugamela as the crucial engagement in Alexander's *anabasis*. However, that near Issus in the northern Levant in November 333 BC is to my mind equally, if not more, important. Here, for the first time, Alexander and the Macedonians fought the King of Kings in person, the latter commanding a full-scale royal army. Yet, despite facing a huge disparity in numbers and relying on highly vulnerable lines of supply, the Macedonian victory was so total that from that point, Alexander's eventual victory seemed the most likely outcome of his campaign.

This was a true epic battle in every sense of the word, and one we know much more about than the Granicus River engagement because the primary sources go into much more detail. Sadly for Darius, the high point of his engagement was the pre-battle strategic manoeuvring, as he then made three tactical errors to confound his earlier seizing of the strategic initiative. First, he killed his best general. This was the Greek *strategos* Charidamus who, on learning of the Macedonian countermarch to intercept the royal army, advised the king to divide his army in two. One, under the Greek general, would tackle Alexander directly, while the other, under Darius, would be held in reserve. However, with his prestige at stake after the Persian defeat at Granicus River, Darius ignored the advice and determined to continue onwards to fight the Macedonians with his entire force. Unfortunately, Charidamus then made the mistake of saying a few ill-chosen words in Greek about the Persians while in Darius' presence. The king, who spoke Greek perfectly, was instantly offended and had the general executed out of hand. In the long run, this clearly proved a major error as, with Memnon already dead after the failed defence of Mytilene, the King of Kings was running out of reliable military advisers.

Then, as his enormous army meandered towards the Macedonians, Darius made his second error. At one point, still some distance from Alexander, he called a halt near a badly positioned Macedonian camp his Bactrian scouts had found. However, far from it being Alexander's main base, it turned out to be a field hospital for those Macedonians still wounded from the Anatolian campaign or suffering from illness. Darius showed no mercy, ordering the execution of many recuperating soldiers, with any allowed to live having their right hand severed. Alexander, already determined to defeat the Persians in a winner takes-all battle, was infuriated and vowed revenge. Darius' final error was his choice of battlefield. Faced with Alexander's advance northwards to force an engagement, he chose a defensive position similar to the satrap's failed defence of the Granicus. This time Darius arrayed his huge army along the Pinaros River, which bisected the coastal plain near Issus. This was a small stream running from the mountains to the north before turning westwards as it met the coastal plain, its route broadly tracking the border today between Turkey and Syria.

At first glance, defending the bank of a waterway, however small, against an attacking opponent certainly gave the Persians a defensive advantage. However, Darius should already have been aware that the Granicus had proved no real obstacle in that engagement given the determination and training of the Macedonians. Further, his key advantage at Issus was weight of numbers, and here the waterway was naturally bounded by the sea to the west and the coastal mountains to the east. Therefore, an envelopment of the Macedonians wasn't an option, and the battle would become a straight fight based on the quality of the various troop types in each army. That gave Alexander an enormous advantage, with Plutarch saying 'Fortune certainly presented Alexander with the ideal terrain for the battle'.[4]

When Alexander's scouts found the Persians ready for battle, the Macedonian king immediately moved to deploy his army out of its column of march into battle array. By this time, he had his full campaigning force with him, totalling over 40,000 men. However, when considering the size of the Persian army, we are again faced with incredible numbers as detailed by the primary sources. For example, Arrian says Darius fielded 600,000 men.[5] Meanwhile, Diodorus Siculus opts for an almost as outrageous 400,000.[6] However, most modern commentators opt for between 60,000 and 120,000. Whatever the actual Persian numbers, Alexander was certainly heavily outnumbered.

This engagement is also notable for the late time of year in which it was fought, in November, reflecting Alexander's propensity for campaigning out of season. In that regard, conditions were notably cold and wet. In terms of deployment, Alexander followed his by-now-standard pattern, with himself on the right with the *ilai* (squadrons) of Companions deployed in their *embolus* (wedge) formations, then moving right to left the Hypaspists, then the phalanx (at least partially under the command of Craterus, promoted after his success commanding a *taxis* of these *pezetairoi* at the Granicus river), and finally Parmenion on the left with the Thessalian and Thracian cavalry. Light troops, including Thracians, Agrianians and Cretans, supported both flanks, while the Macedonian centre was bolstered by allied and mercenary Greek, Illyrian and more Thracian infantry. The Macedonian phalanx deployment here is particularly interesting. As Alexander approached the Pinaros River it was thirty-two men deep, but the king reduced it to eight deep on arrival at the waterway as he sought to extend his centre so as not to leave the extreme flank of the Companions on the right exposed. This meant the bristling deployment of the *pezetairoi* and other heavy foot soldiers alone stretched for over 1.6 km.

Meanwhile, Darius deployed his heavy cavalry next to the coast on his right flank where they could make best use of the broad expanses of flat beach next to the Gulf of Issus, then *kardakes* (Hellenized Persian foot) and next the Greek mercenaries deployed in two large bodies of 15,000 men (both commanded by the *strategos* Thymondas), and finally more *kardakes* and a small number of Median and Hyrcanian cavalry extending the Persian line to the high ground on its extreme left. There Darius stretched his line even further, with some *kardakes* (despite Alexander's best efforts to extend his own line) wrapping around the Macedonian extreme right flank in the foothills. This forced Alexander to match them there in the rough terrain with some of his own elite Agrianian javelinmen. The Persians then deployed a second line comprised of levies behind the troops along the riverbank, no more than a disorganized throng. Finally, Darius positioned himself with his elite guard cavalry between the two bodies of Greek mercenaries to the front. It is noteworthy here that a number of the surviving Persian nobles who'd fought at the Granicus River were also present. These included the former Cilician satrap, Arsames, and also Rheomithres, both deployed with Darius and his guard, both falling in the ensuing battle. Meanwhile, as a final comment on the Persian deployment at Issus, Arrian adds that the foot in the centre (presumably both the Greeks and *kardakes*) reinforced their riverbank defence with 'stockades' where the shoreline was particularly gentle, which he describes elsewhere as 'precipitous'.[7] Polybius describes the same defended riverbank as covered in thorny bushes.[8] Clearly, we are talking here about a significant natural and, with the stockades, man-made obstacle. Both armies now faced off across the Pinarus River. Here Arrian makes a further interesting observation, saying the security of the Persian position actually counted against Darius' army psychologically, with

Alexander believing it indicated inaction, and that therefore Darius was already 'in spirit a beaten man'.[9] This seems harsh, given this was a battle Darius simply needed not to lose, rather than achieve a crushing victory. The Macedonians were already cut off from their lines of supply to the north, and a loss at Issus would have forced Alexander to effect a maritime evacuation across the eastern Mediterranean in waters under Persian control, or head inland or south even further away from safety. Notably, this was the same region where Demetrius was to succumb to Seleucus.

However, Alexander was clearly emboldened by Darius' reticence to engage as he now ordered a general attack across his entire line. One factor here may have been the Macedonian line coming under missile fire from the Persians as soon as it came into range while deploying along the southern riverbank. Again, Alexander led the way, either at the head of a thunderous charge across the Pinaros with his Companions on the right wing, or dismounting with his close guard and leading the Hypaspsists. Interestingly, the word used by Arrian to describe Alexander's initial advance here is *dromo*, meaning at a run. This might suggest he was on foot. However, this seems unlikely given Alexander's swift success on the right, where he quickly broke through the *kardakes* to threaten the Persian centre. The primary sources certainly indicate Darius' left wing was terrified by the speed of Alexander's advance, especially after his Agrianian javelinmen moved to prevent any envelopment by the *kardakes* on the Persian hanging left flank.

However, elsewhere things did not go as well for the Macedonians, with the phalanx unsurprisingly struggling to keep its formation as it crossed the river and navigated the far bank, which as detailed had been fortified where not steep. Here Arrian describes gaps forming between individual phalanx units, presumably the 1,500 strong *taxeis* (see Chapter 1 for detail), with the eight-deep *pezetairoi* suffering at the hands of the Greek mercenary hoplites and Hellenized *kardakes* atop their bank.[10] Indeed, it was only the length of the Macedonian *sarissas* that allowed the pikemen to engage the enemy at all. Soon, Arrian says, 120 Macedonians 'of note' had been slain, this usually interpreted as officers.[11] Meanwhile, any Persian troops armed with missile weapons continued to pour fire into the Macedonian phalanx at point-blank range and, denied the almost unstoppable impetus they enjoyed when on open ground, the *pezetairoi* began to fall back slowly over the Pinarus. Diodorus Siculus says this initial phase of the infantry encounter only lasted a short time, with one interpretation being the Macedonian foot soldiers now began the difficult manoeuvre of disengaging from an enemy to their front.[12] The likelihood of this increases when one considers that the Greek mercenaries and *kardakes* defending their bank were unlikely to pursue given the security of their position, especially with stockades deployed in places across their front. Meanwhile, on the Macedonian left, Parmenion was fairing little better, his outnumbered Thessalian and Greek cavalry rebuffed time and again as they tried to counter Darius' main body of horse. Soon their casualties began to mount and the Persian cavalry began to press them back, Parmenion's horsemen only just holding their line.

However, swift and brutal relief for the Macedonian centre and left was at hand as, just when momentum had been lost there, Alexander smashed through the *kardakes* to his front with the Companions and Hypaspists and, again showing true leadership on the battlefield, instead of pursuing his beaten foe turned left to hammer the now-exposed flank of the Greek mercenaries (in counterpoint to Demetrius at Ipsus). Little resistance was offered given the latter were engaged to their front with the *pezetairoi*, and soon individual men and then small groups of hoplites broke and ran to the rear. Once the integrity of the Greek phalanx was lost, it quickly folded under the combined assault of Alexander's troops and now resurgent pikemen. A savage slaughter ensued, with Alexander then spying Darius and his close guards. Knowing this was his chance to bring the campaign to a swift end, he immediately charged the Persian king. This is the scene some believe is shown in the Alexander Mosaic from the House of the Faun in Pompeii, where the Macedonian king thunders towards Darius in his chariot, *xyston* levelled at the Persian king, the whole montage set against a hedge-like backdrop of waving *sarissas*. However, Darius' brother Oxyathres now intervened, with Quintus Curtius Rufus saying:

> Oxyathres saw Alexander charging Darius and moved his own cavalry right in front of the king's chariot. Oxyathres far surpassed his comrades in the splendour of his arms and in physical strength, and very few could match his courage and devotion to Darius. In that engagement especially he won distinction by cutting down some Macedonians who were recklessly thrusting ahead and putting others to flight.[13]

This bought time for Darius to flee the battlefield with his bodyguard, leaving the Persian army to its fate. This now quickly disintegrated, the better troops to the front hampered in their escape by the levies to their rear. Alexander and the Macedonians pursued until nightfall, with the Persians massacred wherever they were found and little quarter given. Plutarch says that at one point Alexander himself captured Darius' chariot and bow, though the king made good his escape on horseback with around 4,000 cavalry including Oxyathres.[14] The primary sources indicate that the Persians lost up to 100,000 men in the battle (an unlikely figure given the overall size of the army, though certainly Persian losses were very high), with some 8,000 Greek survivors escaping by ship. Meanwhile, Alexander lost 450 dead with around 5,000 wounded. This was a stupendous victory indeed that set the tone for Alexander's forthcoming conquest of Darius' empire. Highlights in the aftermath included his capture of Darius' camp, which included the royal family, with Plutarch enigmatically describing the scene:

> Darius' tent, which was full of splendid furniture and quantities of gold and silver, they [his soldiers] reserved for Alexander himself, who, after he had put off his arms, went to bathe himself saying, 'Let us now cleanse ourselves from the toils of war in the bath of Darius'.[15]

However, despite the scale of his defeat, Darius was still abroad with the vast resources of his remaining empire to call upon. He now resolved to fight on, this time through his surrogates, with Alexander's next major engagements taking place on the Levantine coast. The final confrontation would come soon enough though, in one of the greatest battles of the ancient world.

The Battle of Gaugamela

All was now set for the final encounter between Alexander and Darius, which took place on 1 October 331 BC. In terms of the armies engaged, Alexander fielded the full 47,000 men available to him, this proportionally similar to his earlier though smaller armies at the Granicus River and Issus, with his Companions, *prodromoi*, Thessalian and Greek heavy horse, Thracian and Paeonian light horse, Hypaspists, *pezetairoi*, Greek allied and mercenary foot troops, Thracians, Illyrians, Agrianians and Cretans. However, as usual, there is far more debate about the size of Darius' army among the primary sources, and subsequently. Most modern sources settle for a figure between 250,000 and 300,000 in Darius' army. In particular, given much of the Persian army was recruited in the east, Darius had a huge advantage in the number of cavalry. This disparity in mounted troops certainly precluded a Macedonian disengagement once battle was joined, a fact which clearly influenced Alexander's approach to the battle. Further, the Persian army included 200 scythed chariots, while its Indian contingent also had 15 elephants.

In terms of the Macedonian order of battle, Alexander was at the height of his tactical genius here, ordering a particularly complex deployment only possible for the most disciplined and motivated of armies. His centre was deployed in echelon in two lines to prevent an encirclement, the Macedonian phalanx to the fore under Craterus, with the Hypaspists the furthest forward on their right under Parmenion's son Nicanor, with the Greek allies and mercenaries then deployed to the rear. The latter were positioned to allow an about-face if the army was enveloped. Meanwhile, Alexander once more commanded his own shock cavalry to the right of the Hypaspists, including all six *ilai* of the Companions in their wedge formations. Meanwhile, Parmenion again commanded the left. His wing, deployed furthest from the Persians in the oblique set-up, included the Thessalian and Thracian cavalry, and more heavy foot soldiers. Additionally, floating units of cavalry and light troops covered the flanks and rear of both wings, with the *prodromoi* on the extreme right.

The exact deployment of Darius' vast army eludes us today, though it likely comprised a rolling front of various types of cavalry stretching from horizon to horizon, intermingled with the better foot soldiers, and with the huge numbers of levies to the rear. Once more, as the battle unfolded, the latter's main role would be to obstruct Darius' better troops once his army broke. We do have some detail here and there from the primary sources that give a flavour of the colourful composition of the King of King's army. For example, Darius in his chariot positioned himself in his accustomed position in the exact centre, with his close relatives, royal guard cavalry and royal foot guards in attendance. Either side were the Greek mercenaries, with 100 of the scythed chariots deployed across their front. Nearby were some of the Indian contingent including the fifteen elephants, Carians (presumably refugees from the region in Anatolia) and Iranian cavalry. Meanwhile, behind Darius in a hollow could be found the Babylonian and Red Sea contingents, these most likely levy foot soldiers given their position to the rear. Mazaeus, the former satrap of Cilicia, commanded the right-wing cavalry, including large contingents of Syrians, Mesopotamians, Medes, Parthians, Saka, Tapurians, Hyrcanians, Albanians (from the Caucasus), Sacasinians, Cappadocians, Armenians and fifty scythed chariots.

Meanwhile Bessus, satrap of Bactria and a close relative of Darius, commanded the Persian left wing facing Alexander on the Macedonian right, his force including more members of the royal family, Bactrians, Dahae and more Saka, together with fifty more scythed chariots. Less is known about the actual battle, though most primary sources suggest Alexander opened the engagement with a general advance which maintained his oblique formation, with the centre still deployed in its two lines. This placed the Hypaspists and Companions furthest forward on the right, with the king to the fore.

This makes sense given the huge disparity in numbers, with Alexander knowing time was against him and that his quickest route to victory was to target Darius directly. It also replicated his success at Issus, with his plan to use the best troops under his own leadership to punch through the enemy battleline while the latter was pinned by the *pezetairoi* in true later Argead 'hammer-and-anvil' fashion. One can envisage the Macedonians here advancing in an offset rhomboid, with the front right corner furthest forward, moving at speed towards a seemingly endless line of Persians to their front. Darius responded quickly, matching Alexander's aggression with a general advance of his own. This meant that soon both of his wings easily overlapped the Macedonian formation. However, he quickly realized that the Companions and Hypaspists were moving so quickly that they would likely impact his battleline near his own position before his army could effect the planned envelopment. He therefore ordered Bessus and his eastern horsemen on the left wing to speed their own advance so as to wrap around the Macedonian right wing to slow them. This managed to push back the Macedonian right-wing flank cover, with more and more Persian cavalry then joining Bessus to reinforce his initial success.

Meanwhile in the centre, Darius now launched his scythed chariots against the *pezetairoi*, hoping to at least disrupt the Macedonian pikemen before they could impact the Persian battleline. However, as usual the chariots proved a spectacular failure, with most shot down by Alexander's skirmishers and those reaching the phalanx refusing to charge the hedge of pikes, instead being driven down lanes deliberately opened between the units of *pezetairoi* to their doom. Soon the phalanx resumed its advance and began pressing the mercenary hoplites and foot guards to Darius' front. The 'anvil' was now in position.

On the Macedonian right wing, Alexander noted the thinning of the Persian left wing as more and more of Bessus' cavalry, and now mounted troops from the Persian centre, began to lap around his extreme right wing. Soon a gap had opened up in the Persian line and Alexander pounced, the 'hammer' charging through at full pelt with the king at the head of the Companions, supported by those units of the Hypaspists who could keep up and unengaged units of the phalanx. This attack punched through the Persian royal guard cavalry, exposing Darius himself. The King of Kings then fled again, rather than stand and fight. Alexander pursued vigorously, wanting to finish things there and then.

However, on the Macedonian left Parmenion had been under pressure for some time with Mazaeus' huge cavalry wing attacking in repeating waves. Indeed, some Persian cavalry had actually reached the Macedonian baggage camp where they killed the camp guard and freed a large number of Persian prisoners. The *strategos* now sent word to Alexander, requesting support to prevent his wing being overrun. The primary sources differ here on the Macedonian king's response, with Diodorus Siculus saying the courier couldn't find Alexander who was too far ahead in his pursuit of Darius.[16] However, Arrian says Alexander received the report and, hugely frustrated, broke off his pursuit and headed back to help Parmenion. On the way though, his force met some returning Persian cavalry including Parthians and Saka, and a desperate melee ensued. According to Arrian, this was some of the heaviest fighting Alexander experienced in the entire battle, with sixty companions killed and many more wounded, including Hephaestion.[17] Anticlimactically, by the time they reached Parmenion, his left wing had been secured, and it seems likely the cavalry Alexander met, if Arrian is correct, were Mazaeus' troops withdrawing after word reached them of Darius' wretched escape.

By this time, the Macedonian success on the right had enabled the rest of the army to roll up what remained of the demoralized Persian centre. The vast army now finally broke, with Alexander again in the van leading a vigorous pursuit. Once more a huge slaughter ensued, with various contemporary reports saying the Persians lost between 40,000 and 300,000 dead depending on the source, and the Macedonians an equally unlikely 100 to 500.

Sadly for Alexander, Darius escaped with some Bactrian cavalry and Greek mercenaries, fleeing northeast to Media. The Macedonians pursued for a number of days until they lost contact. Alexander then occupied Babylonia and reinstalled Mazaeus as the regional satrap in Babylon, recognising the Persian's leadership and bravery at Gaugamela. Thus ended Alexander's greatest battle, and soon his *anabasis* was underway once more, with India beckoning after the later death of Darius.

The Battle of the Hydaspes River

Alexander's final set-piece battle took place in the context of his support for the Indian king Taxiles, with his great rival Porus quickly moving against the Macedonians when he learned of it. In typical fashion Alexander immediately countered, seeking a meeting engagement as soon as possible. He built a fortified camp near a local town, thought to be modern Jhelum, as his base of operations.

In the spring of 326 BC, Alexander learned that Porus had drawn up his army on the south bank of the nearby Hydaspes River to counter any crossing by the Macedonians. This was a significant waterway, deep and fast enough to prevent any crossing attempt except by a significant ford. Arriving at the river, Alexander began to scout the north bank each night with his mounted troops, looking for a suitable ford. However, every time they found a candidate site to cross, Porus arrived to deter them. Finally, in early May, the Macedonians found a suitable crossing 27 km downstream of their camp where a forest-covered island (some sources call this Admana Island) sat in the middle of a meandering bend in the river. The current here was unusually sluggish, allowing Alexander to use the transport vessels his pioneers had ready to assemble to ferry his army across when all was ready. However, he knew that transporting such a huge force across the river would quickly draw Porus' attention. Then, if the Indian army arrived before he could get his army fully across to the southern bank, he'd be forced to fight a defended river-crossing battle yet again. This would most likely spell disaster given that the Hydaspes, even here at the island meander, was a far more significant waterway than either the Granicus or Pinarus.

Alexander now employed a stratagem to put Porus off his guard. Instead of crossing directly, he noisily paraded mounted troops up and down the northern bank of the Hydaspes each evening within earshot of Porus' troops. The Indian king took the bait, on successive nights deploying for battle much of his army including his elephants in case the Macedonians really did cross. Eventually, after repeated nocturnal false alarms, Porus relaxed his guard and stopped responding to the Macedonian cavalry on the far bank given, as Arrian details, he was 'no longer expecting a sudden attempt under cover of darkness, and was lulled into a sense of security'.[18] Then Alexander pounced.

On the appointed night, the assembled ferrying fleet was readied on the northern bank of the Hydaspes by the engineers, this comprising thirty oared galleys, smaller vessels 'cut in half' and skins filled with hay.[19] Alexander was now faced with a dilemma, knowing he couldn't ferry his entire army over in one night, and that the following morning Porus would quickly become aware of the crossing and counter it. The Macedonian king therefore devised a classic pincer tactic strategy, first leading much of his cavalry and some foot troops across to pin the Indians in place while, later, the rest of his army would cross to secure the victory. The latter were split into in two divisions. The first, under Craterus, featured two *taxeis* of *pezetairoi*, 5,000 Indian allies and some allied cavalry. These initially stayed in the Macedonian camp. Meanwhile the second division, under Meleager, featured three *taxeis* of the phalanx and some mercenaries. Deployed a few kilometres upstream from Alexander, but short of the camp and Craterus, Meleager's command had orders to cross the Hydaspes first when the king sent word, with Craterus to follow after. Attalus and Gorgias acted as the key subordinates.

Alexander's assault force comprised 5,000 cavalry and 6,000 foot soldiers. The former included the four *hipparchies* of Companions (the first including the king's 300-strong *agema* of royal guards as the Royal Squadron were now commonly known), plus newly recruited allied and mercenary cavalry from Bactria, Sogdiana, the Saka and the Dahae. Meanwhile his foot soldiers comprised the Argyraspides (as the Hypaspists were now known), two *taxeis* of the phalanx, his Cretans and the Agrianians. Alexander now began his crossing to south bank of the Hydaspes, bypassing the island to his immediate west, with the cavalry mounts on the galleys and boats, while many of his foot soldiers waded across. The king himself led the way standing in the prow of a triaconter, the smallest class of war galley, though the largest he had available. Plutarch here makes reference to the atrocious night-time conditions of the crossing, saying:

> Here he was overtaken by tremendous bursts of thunder and lightning. Although he saw that a number of his men were struck dead by the lightning, he continued the advance and made for the opposite bank. After the storm, the Hydaspes, which was roaring down in high flood, had scooped out a deep channel, so that much of the stream was diverted to this direction and the ground between the two currents had become broken and slippery and made it impossible for his men to gain a firm footing.[20]

It was on this occasion that Alexander is said (by Plutarch) to have exclaimed, 'O Athenians, will you ever believe what risks I am running just to earn your praise'.[21] However, on landing on the opposite shore, the Macedonians realized they had made a mistake, because far from landing on the southern shore they found that instead they had arrived on the banks of a smaller, though still treacherous, branch of the Hydaspes, this error showing how heavily wooded the banks actually were. This meant yet another crossing to reach Porus' side of the river. This Alexander achieved, though not without a huge amount of effort, and by the time he had gathered his crossing force ready for action the sun was high in the sky and Porus had had time to respond. This was in the form of an armed reconnaissance comprising 120 heavy chariots and 4,000 cavalry under the command of Porus' son. However, as they approached Alexander, they came under sustained mounted bow fire from the Bactrians, Sogdians, Saka and Dahae light horse, followed by a headlong charge by Alexander leading the *agema* and other Companions.[22]

The Indian force was completely routed, with many of the chariots abandoned in the soft mud along the shoreline. Plutarch says they left 400 dead behind, including the king's son.[23] Soon news reached Porus of the death of his son and the failure of the chariots and cavalry to push Alexander back over the Hydaspes. Aware the main engagement was now imminent, he deployed his army accordingly. This followed the standard practice as detailed in the Arthaśāstra treatise on military strategy, with the Indian cavalry on the wings, fronted by heavy chariots, and the infantry in the centre with the elephants stretched across their front. The Indian king, clad in chainmail and riding his tallest war elephant (described by Plutarch as highly intelligent and paying great attention to Porus' safety[24]), chose a broad riparian plain for the engagement to allow his chariots the best chance of success given their earlier issues facing Alexander's crossing force. He also left behind a small force of elephants and poor-quality infantry to face Craterus if he attempted to cross the Hydaspes from the Macedonian camp. Finally, it seems Porus also kept to his rear a reserve of poor-quality foot soldiers, most likely local levies. The primary sources all detail the bright spectacle on display across the ranks of the Indian front-line troops, with multi-coloured shields, hauberks, cloaks and scarves, the bowmen poised with long iron-tipped arrows at the ready. One can also imagine the cacophony of noise from the elephants, and the trumpets and bells used to signal Indian troop movements across the battlefield.

The primary sources all emphasize the smaller scale of Porus' army at the Hydaspes compared to the enormous forces earlier deployed by Darius. We have more insight into the size of the army Alexander fielded in the main engagement, if only because we have detail about individual unit sizes in the Macedonian army. This included the troops Alexander had initially led across the river and Meleager's force that had by this time crossed the Hydaspes, most likely after the king had engaged the younger Porus' blocking force, though it is unclear where the crossing was actually made. Craterus' troops in the Macedonian camp set out to join Alexander when battle was about to be joined but arrived too late to participate, later joining in the pursuit of the

Indian army. Some estimate that Alexander's overall force for the main engagement was around 18,000 strong, though given the king's total force for his invasion of the Punjab numbered around 52,000, his army at the Hydaspes was probably considerably larger, and certainly bigger than that of Porus.

Piecing together the various isolated details of Alexander's deployment at the Hydaspes in the primary sources, a reasonable recreation places the king with the *agema*, Companions, allied and mercenary cavalry on the right wing, then the Argyraspides, phalanx and Greek allies and mercenaries in the centre (in that order right to left) and the Thracian and Paeonian light horse on the left wing. A cloud of light foot soldiers, including the Cretans (to the right) and Agrianians (to the right centre), were deployed across the front of the army. It is unclear where the *prodromoi* were positioned, though most likely they were with Alexander and the companions. Finally, in the last minutes before battle commenced, the king detached a unit of Companions under Coenus (it is unclear how many, though no more than a *hipparchia*) from his right wing to support his left-wing light cavalry, having seen more Indian cavalry arrive opposite them at the last minute.

Battle commenced in the sweltering Indian afternoon with Alexander ordering his allied cavalry on the right, led by the Dahae, to harass the Indians to their front. A thundering charge by the Companions led by Alexander himself then followed, which left the Indian left-wing chariots and cavalry on the point of breaking. Seeing this, Porus countered by sending some of his right-wing chariots and horse to support his left wing. However, as they arrived, the newly approaching Coenus on the Macedonian left spurred his companions to follow the departing Indians opposite and soon the reinforced Indian mounted troops on the left found themselves fighting Alexander to their front and Coenus to their rear. The Indian cavalry tried to form a double-facing line to tackle the dual threat but lacked the training and soon the whole left wing broke under the Macedonian onslaught.

Some of the Indian horse fled to the safety of the elephants deployed across the front of the Indian centre. Seeing this, Alexander ordered the Argyraspides, phalanx and Greek allies and mercenaries in the centre to advance, aiming to taken advantage of the state of confusion to their front, caused by the retreating Indian cavalry as they mingled with the elephants and Indian foot soldiers. Porus then ordered his elephants to charge *en masse* though the milling Indian cavalry, and soon a titanic clash ensued as they smashed into the Macedonian heavy foot soldiers in the centre. At first the powerful beasts caused heavy losses among the pikemen and spearmen, their armour-clad tusks impaling many men. Others were tossed in the air, only to be crushed under foot by the elephants when they landed. However, under great duress, the Macedonian centre held and soon their pikes and spears were causing heavy casualties among the Indian elephant crews. Meanwhile, the Cretan, Agrianian and other Macedonian skirmishers began harassing the beasts with their bows, javelins and slings, aiming at the eyes of the elephants, and again their crews. Then re-armed *pezetairoi* emerged from the ranks of the heavy infantry equipped with heavy axes, bravely weaving in and out of the stamping elephant feet to chop at their hamstrings. Soon many of the wounded and crewless beasts were panicking, with one after another fleeing back towards their own lines. There chaos ensued as the elephants ran amok among their own cavalry and infantry. The Macedonian heavy foot troops now reformed, with the Argyraspides and *pezetairoi* adopting the *synaspismos* (locked-shield formation) and advancing on the confused, thrashing mass of elephants, horses and men to their front. Once more the 'anvil' was set in place as they drove all before them backwards, advancing step by step. Meanwhile, Alexander led the Companions and other Macedonian cavalry in a devastating charge into the rear of the Indian centre, with the 'hammer' once again winning the battle. The Indian army quickly broke, with Craterus and his men then arriving to join the pursuit.

Porus himself was soon captured, though he only agreed to surrender when overcome by thirst, with Alexander riding out to meet him and treating him as a celebrated and worthy foe. In terms of losses, Arrian says the Indians lost around 23,000 men, while Diodorus Siculus details 12,000 dead and 9,000 captured.[25] Porus also lost another son, while his ally Spitakes was also killed, and most of his nobles. Alexander captured eighty elephants on the battlefield, and intercepted seventy more as they arrived to reinforce Porus' now defeated army. Meanwhile, Arrian adds Macedonian losses amounted to eighty infantry, twenty Companions, ten allied horse archers and 200 other horse troops.[26] Diodorus Siculus gives a more reasonable 1,000 Macedonian dead, this easily believable after the initial clash between Porus' elephants and the Macedonian centre.[27]

Notes and References

Introduction

1. Diodorus Siculus, *Library of History*, 45.1.
2. J. Romm, *Demetrius, Sacker of Cities* (New Haven, 2022), p. 91.

Chapter 1

1. Simon Hornblower and Anthony Spawforth (Oxford, 1996) p. 1153.
2. *Ibid.*
3. Thucydides, *The Peloponnesian War*, V.68.
4. Xenophon, *Constitution of the Lacedemonians.* 11
5. Tyrtaeus, *Greek Elegiac Poetry*, 21-38 of fragment 11.
6. *Ibid.*
7. Polybius, *The Rise of the Roman Empire*, 18.28-32.
8. Christopher Matthew, *An Invincible Beast* (Barnsley, 2015), p. 206.
9. Asclepiodotus, *Tactics*, trans by W. A. Oldfather and C. H. Oldfather (London and New York, 1923).
10. Plutarch, *Lives*, Aemilius, 19.
11. Arrian, *Anabasis Alexandri*, 4.30.5 and 5.23.7.
12. Quintus Curtius Rufus, *The History of Alexander*, 8.1.3.
13. Arrian, *Anabasis,* 7.11.3.
14. David Karunanithy, *The Macedonian War* Machine (Barnsley, 2013), p. 117
15. Quintus Curtius Rufus, *The History of Alexander*, 5.2.10.
16. Diodorus Siculus, *Library of History*, 18.27.
17. Romm, Demetrius, p. 112.

Chapter 2

1. J. Haywood, *Cassell Atlas of the Classical World 500 BC – AD 600* (London, 1998), p. 208.
2. Peter Green, *Alexander to Actium* (Oakland, 1993), p.5.
3. Robin Lane Fox, *Alexander the Great*, (London, 2004), p. 28
4. Adrian Goldsworthy, *Philip and Alexander* (2020), p. 15.
5. Plutarch, *Lives*, Alexander, 6.5.
6. Diodorus Siculus, *Library of History,* 16.86.
7. Plutarch, *Lives*, Alexander, 9.1.
8. Aelian, *Historical Miscellany*, 12.43.
9. Justin, *Epitome*, 16.1
10. Plutarch, *Lives*, Phocion, 2.2.
11. Xenophon, *Anabasis*, 1.6.

12. Quintus Curtius Rufus, *The History of Alexander*, 3.1.
13. Diodorus Siculus, *Library of History,* 17.100.
14. Plutarch, *Parallel Lives*, Demetrius, 2.1.
15. Romm, *Demetrius,* p. 3.
16. Plutarch, *Lives*, Demetrius, 3.1.
17. Romm, *Demetrius,* p. 12.
18. Plutarch, *Lives*, Alexander, 4.10.
19. Plutarch, *Lives*, Alexander, 4.11.
20. Plutarch, *Lives*, Alexander, 49.121.
21. Arrian, A*nabasis,* 4.7.3).
22. Arrian, *Anabasis*, 4.8.9; Plutarch, *Lives,* Alexander, 50.126.
23. Plutarch, *Lives*, Alexander, 55.136.
24. Arrian, *Anabasis*, 7.8.3.

Chapter 3

1. Diodorus Siculus, *Library of History,* 18.1.
2. Green, *Alexander to Actium*, p. 81.
3. Plutarch, *Lives*, Eumenes, 3.1.
4. Diodorus Siculus, *Library of History*, 18.23.
5. Polyaenus, *Stratagems*, 4.6.
6. Diodorus Siculus, *Library of History*, 18.39.
7. Plutarch, *Lives*, Demetrius, 20.4.
8. *Ibid.*
9. Romm, *Demetrius,* p. 13.
10. Polyaenus, *Stratagems*, 4.6.
11. Diodorus Siculus, *Library of History*, 18.4.
12. *Ibid.*
13. Diodorus Siculus, *Library of History*, 18.5; Plutarch, *Lives*, Eumenes, 12.1.
14. Plutarch, *Lives*, Eumenes, 13.1.
15. Polyaenus, *Stratagems*, 4.6.
16. *Ibid.*
17. Diodorus Siculus, *Library of History*, 19.4
18. Diodorus Siculus, *Library of History*, 19.43
19. Polyaenus, *Stratagems*, 4.6.13.
20. Plutarch, *Lives*, Eumenes, 18.

Chapter 4

1. Romm, *Demetrius*, p. 29.
2. Plutarch, *Lives*, Demetrius, 54.
3. Plutarch, *Lives*, Demetrius, 6.1.
4. Plutarch, *Lives*, Demetrius, 6.1.
5. P. Wheatley, The Implications of 'Poliorcetes': Was Demetrius the Besieger's Nickname Ironic? *Histos*. Vol 14, 152 (2020), p. 162.
6. Plutarch, *Lives*, Demetrius, 631.
7. Diodorus Siculus, *Library of History*, 20.4.

8. Diodorus Siculus, *Library of History*, 20.1.
9. Plutarch, *Lives*, Demetrius, 6.3.
10. Athenaeus, *The Learned Banqueters*, 524B.
11. Diodorus Siculus, *Library of History*, 20.4.
12. Polyaenus, *Stratagems*, 4.7.
13. Plutarch, *Lives*, Demetrius, 9.
14. Romm, *Demetrius*, p. 51.
15. Plutarch, *Lives*, Demetrius, 9.
16. Diodorus Siculus, *Library of History*, 51.1.
17. Romm, *Demetrius*, p. 61.
18. Diodorus Siculus, *Library of History*, 91.1.
19. Diodorus Siculus, *Library of History*, 93.1.
20. Diodorus Siculus, *Library of History*, 94.1.
21. Diodorus Siculus, *Library of History*, 95.1.
22. Diodorus Siculus, *Library of History*, 96.1.
23. Diodorus Siculus, *Library of History*, 95.1.
24. Diodorus Siculus, *Library of History*, 20.103.
25. Plutarch, *Lives*, Demetrius, 29.3.

Chapter 5

1. A. B. Bosworth, *The Legacy of Alexander: Politics, Warfare, and Propaganda under the Successors* (Oxford: 2002), p. 247).
2. Plutarch, *Lives*, Demetrius, 30.2.
3. Plutarch, *Lives*, Demetrius, 31.2.
4. *Ibid.*
5. Plutarch, *Lives*, Demetrius, 42.1.
6. Romm, *Demetrius*, p. 155.
7. Plutarch, *Lives*, Demetrius, 46.4.
8. Romm, *Demetrius*, p.159.

Appendix A

1. Pausanius, *Guide to Greece*, 9.7.2.
2. Athenaeus, *The Learned Banqueters*, 1.18.
3. Justin, *Epitome*, 13.4.

Appendix B

1. Diodorus Siculus, *Library of History*, 17.19.
2. Arrian, *Anabasis*, 1.13.
3. Plutarch, *Lives*, Alexander, 16.14.
4. Plutarch, *Lives*, Alexander, 20.
5. Arrian, *Anabasis*, 2.8.6
6. Diodorus Siculus, *Library of History*, 17.19.
7. Arrian, *Anabasis*, 2.10.
8. Polybius, 12.22.
9. Arrian, *Anabasis*, 2.10.2.

10. Arrian, *Anabasis*, 2.10.1.
11. Arrian, *Anabasis*, 2.10.3.
12. Diodorus Siculus, *Library of History*, 17.33.
13. Quintus Curtius Rufus, *The History of Alexander*, 3.11.8.
14. Plutarch, *Lives*, Alexander, 20.2.
15. *Ibid.*
16. Diodorus Siculus, *Library of History*, 17.53.
17. Arrian, *Anabasis*, 3.8.
18. Arrian, *Anabasis*, 5.15.
19. Arrian, *Anabasis*, 5.18.
20. Plutarch, *Lives*, Alexander, 60.
21. *Ibid.*
22. Arrian, *Anabasis*, 5.15.
23. Plutarch, *Lives*, Alexander, 60.
24. *Ibid.*
25. Arrian, *Anabasis*, 5.18; Diodorus Siculus, *Library of History*, 17.89.1.
26. Arrian, *Anabasis*, 5.18.
27. Diodorus Siculus, *Library of History*, 17.89.1.

Bibliography

Ancient Sources

Aelian, *Historical Miscellany*. 1997. Wilson, N. G., Harvard: Loeb Classical Library.

Arrian, *Anabasis Alexandri*. 1989. Brunt, P. A., Harvard: Loeb Classical Library.

Asclepiodotus, *Tactics* (London and New York, 1923).

Athenaeus, *The Learned Banqueters*. 2007. Olson, S. D., Harvard: Loeb Classical Library.

Cassius Dio, *Roman History*. 1925. Cary, E., Harvard: Loeb Classical Library.

Diodorus Siculus, *Library of History*, Volume 3. 1939. Oldfather, C.H., Harvard: Loeb Classical Library.

Herodian, *History of the Roman Empire*. 1989. Whittaker, C. R., Harvard: Loeb Classical Library.

Herodotus, *The Histories*. 2003. De Selincourt, A., London: Penguin.

Homer, *The Iliad*. 1950. Rieu, E.V., London: Penguin.

Justin, *Epitome of the Philippic History of Pompeius Trogus*. 1994. Yardley, J. C., Oxford: Oxford University Press.

Livy, *The History of Rome*. 1989. Foster, B. O. Cambridge, MA: Harvard University Press/ Loeb Classical Library.

Pausanias, *Guide Greece: Central Greece*. 1979. Levi, P., London: Penguin.

Pliny the Elder, *Natural History*. 1940. Rackham, H., Harvard: Harvard University Press.

Pliny the Younger, *Epistularum Libri Decem*. 1963, Mynors, R.A.B., Oxford: Oxford Classical Texts – Clarendon Press.

Plutarch, *Lives of the Noble Greeks and Romans*. 2013. Clough, A. H. Oxford. Benediction Classics.

Plutarch, *Plutarch's Morals*. 1874. Goodwin, W. W. Cambridge: Little, Brown and Company.

Polybius, *The Rise of the Roman Empire*. 1979, Scott-Kilvert, I., London: Penguin.

Quintus Curtius Rufus, *The History of Alexander*. 2003. Heckel, W., London: Penguin.

Strabo, *The Geography*. 2014, Roler, D.W., Cambridge: Cambridge University Press.

Thucyides, *The History of the Peloponnesian War*. 2000. Warner, R., London: Penguin.

Tyrtaeus, *Greek Elegiac Poetry*. 1999. Gerber, D. E. Loeb Classical Library.

Xenophon, *Cyropaedia: The Education of Cyrus*. 2017. Dakyns, H. G., Scotts Valley, California: CreateSpace Independent Publishing Platform.

Xenophon, *Anabasis*. 2017. Warner, R., London: Penguin.

Modern Sources

Bennett, B. and Roberts, M. 2008. *The Wars of Alexander's Successors 323–281 BC*. Barnsley: Pen & Sword.

Bosworth, A. B. 2002. *The Legacy of Alexander: Politics, Warfare, and Propaganda under the Successors*. Oxford: Oxford University Press.

Brooke, A. 2005. Alexander the Great – or the Terrible. *The Hudson Review*. Vol 58, 220 -230.
Connolly, P. 1988. *Greece and Rome at War.* London: Macdonald & Co (Publishers) Ltd.
Cornell, T. J. and Matthews, J. 1982. *Atlas of the Roman World.* Oxford: Phaidon Press Ltd.
Cowan, R. 2003a. *Roman Legionary, 58 BC – AD 69.* Oxford: Osprey Publishing.
Cunliffe, B. 1988. *Greeks, Romans and Barbarians. Spheres of Interaction.* London: Batsford Ltd.
Dowley, T. 1997. *The Atlas of the Bible and Christianity.* Oxford: Candle books.
Elliott, S. 2021. *Ancient Greeks at War.* Oxford: Casemate Publishers.
Erdkamp, P. ed. 2013. *The Cambridge Companion to Ancient Rome.* Cambridge. Cambridge University Press.
Goldsworthy, A. 2020. *Philip and Alexander.* London: Apollo.
Golvin, J. C. 2003. *Ancient Cities Brought to Life.* Ludlow: Thalamus Publishing.
Green, P. 1993. *Alexander to Actium.* Oakland: California University Press.
Haywood, J. 1998. *Cassell Atlas of the Classical World 500 BC – AD 600.* London: Cassell plc.
Holland, T. 2005. *Persian Fire.* London: Abacus.
Hornblower, S. and Spawforth, A. 1996. *The Oxford Classical Dictionary.* Oxford: Oxford University Press.
James, S. 2011. *Rome and the Sword.* London: Thames and Hudson.
Karunanithy, D. 2013. *The Macedonian War Machine.* Barnsley: Pen & Sword.
Lane Fox, R. 2004. *Alexander the Great.* London: Penguin.
Matthew, C. 2015. *An Invincible Beast: Understanding the Hellenistic Pike Phalanx in Action.* Barnsley: Pen & Sword.
Matyszak, P. 2009. *Roman Conquests: Macedonia and Greece.* Barnsley: Pen & Sword.
Romm, J. 2022. *Demetrius: Sacker of Cities.* New Haven: Yale University Press.
Spawforth, T. 2018. *The Story of Greece and Rome.* New Haven: Yale University Press.
Wheatley, P. 2020. The Implications of 'Poliorcetes': Was Demetrius the Besieger's Nickname Ironic? *Histos.* Vol 14, 152 184.
Wilson, I. 1999. *The Bible of History.* London: Weidenfeld & Nicholson.

Index